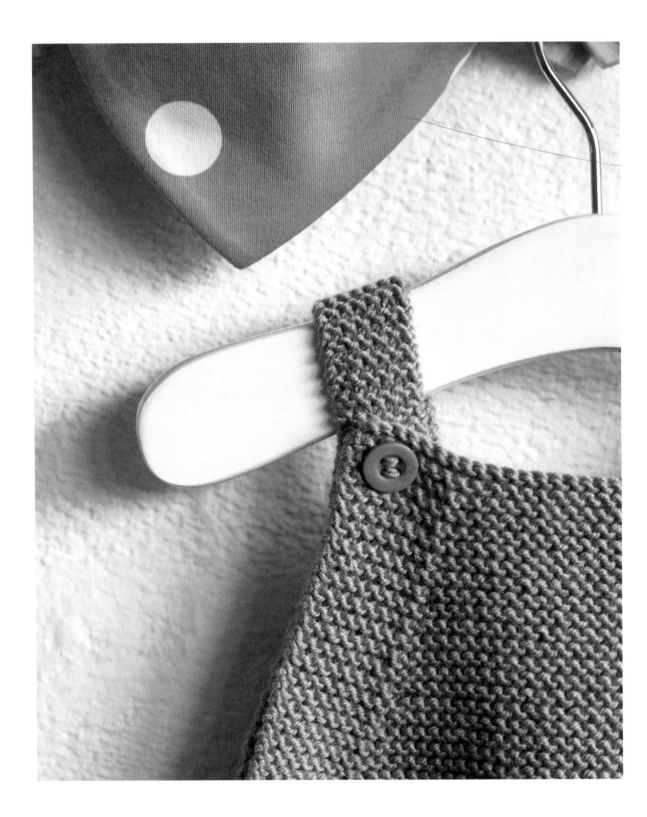

BABY'S FIRST KNITS

20 Irresistible Knits for Babies

Debbie Bliss

Photography by Ola Smit

DOVER PUBLICATIONS, INC.
Mineola, New York

CONTENTS

INTRODUCTION

I am often asked what I knit for pleasure and the answer is always the same—items for babies. As so much of my time professionally is taken up with creating fashion knits for my collections, in my spare time I like to have a project on the go that has no deadline—other than an imminent birth! I tend to go for an easy-to-knit classic; simple because I want it to be as relaxing as possible to knit, and classic because then I know I can't go wrong—I don't want to predict the taste and style of the person I am giving it to.

For new knitters a baby project is perfect. It's small and quick to knit so you are rewarded by a finished piece before you lose heart if you are struggling with new techniques. And, of course, it has the bonus of knowing that the time and effort you have put into it has created something special.

I designed the projects in *Baby's First Knits* to reflect the different stages as you learn to knit, from the absolute basics such as casting on, to the more advanced techniques of cabling and Fair Isle. Each new technique has step-by-step instructions to ease you into the craft and build your confidence. Hopefully this collection will not only be useful for beginners, but also for knitters who want to brush up on or learn a new technique, or who just enjoy simple styles that don't go out of fashion.

I have chosen soft fibers, with cashmere blends, beautiful merinos and an organic cotton—all yarns that are gentle against a baby's or child's skin. The knits include the most basic of blankets for a starter project and also my favorite styles—a practical hooded sweater and a smart double-breasted coat—so I hope there is plenty for you to enjoy and make.

HOW TO USE THIS BOOK

This book has been carefully planned to build up a new knitter's skills through creating beautiful hand-knitted items. Read this section before you start knitting to help you get the most from the patterns and techniques.

In the first section of this book, from pages 11–27, you will find basic information on different aspects of knitting, and it is well worth familiarizing yourself with all of this if you are a complete beginner, or if you haven't picked up needles and yarn in quite a while.

As well as sections on yarns and equipment, you'll also find useful advice on reading and understanding the knitting patterns in the book, including a full list of the abbreviations used in the projects.

This book primarily uses US (UK) methods of holding the yarn and needles, and they are shown in this section. However, the Continental method is a popular alternative and instructions for that are given on pages 24–26. If you are left-handed you may find these techniques easier to use than the US (UK) methods.

Each project introduces new skills, and each new skill has step-by-step instructions to show you exactly how to work it. The project knitting pattern contains cross-references to the new techniques, which appear on the pages following the pattern. So if you are unsure how to

work a technique, just turn to the instructions. However, if you have already mastered a skill, you can follow the pattern without interruption.

Some techniques are shown on two different knitted fabrics so that you can clearly understand them within the context of a particular project. There are also cross-referenced Pattern Notes that give helpful tips and advice on different aspects of a pattern.

The techniques

Here is an alphabetical list of all the techniques taught in this book, plus the Pattern Notes, with the numbers of the pages you will find them on if you need to refer back to something.

YARNS

When choosing a yarn for babies or children, it is essential that you work with a fiber that is soft and gentle against a baby's skin. Babies are not able to tell you if a collar is rough against their neck or if cuffs are irritating their wrists, and as older children are often more used to the lightweight freedom of fleeces, they can be resistant to hand-knits that they may consider scratchy and uncomfortable.

The yarns I have chosen for the patterns in this book are cashmere combined with merino wool—giving softness and durability—a pure wool and a pure cotton. Although they create fabrics that are sumptuously soft to wear, most importantly all these yarns are machine washable.

When knitting a garment, whenever possible do use the yarn stated in the pattern. All these designs have been created with a specific yarn in mind: the pants (page 48) are worked in a cashmere blend so that the fabric is soft against a baby's legs, while the coat (page 92) is made in a merino wool to give it the necessary sturdiness for an outerwear jacket and to maintain its shape—a floppier fiber or a synthetic yarn would create a limp fabric. From an aesthetic point of view, the clarity of a subtle stitch pattern such as seed stitch may be lost if knitted in an inferior yarn.

Here are descriptions of my yarns used in this book and a guide to their weights and types.

Debbie Bliss Baby Cashmerino
A lightweight yarn between a sport weight and a double knitting: 55% merino wool, 33% microfiber, 12% cashmere
Approximately 137yd per 1¾oz (50g) ball

Debbie Bliss Cashmerino Aran
55% merino wool, 33% microfiber, 12% cashmere
Approximately 98yd per 1¾oz (50g) ball

Debbie Bliss Rialto DK
100% merino wool
Approximately 115yd per 1¾oz (50g) ball

Debbie Bliss Eco Baby
100% cotton
Approximately 137yd per 1¾oz (50g) ball

Buying yarn

The ball band on the yarn will carry all the essential information you need as to gauge, needle size, weight and yardage. Importantly it will also have the dye lot. Yarns are dyed in batches or lots, which can vary considerably. As your retailer may not have the same dye lot later on, buy all your yarn for a project at the same time. If you know that sometimes you use more yarn than that quoted in the pattern, buy extra. If it is not possible to buy all the yarn you need with the same dye lot, use the different ones where it will not show as much—on a neck or border for example—as a change of dye lot across a main piece will most likely show.

It is also a good idea at the time of buying the yarn to check the pattern and make sure that you already have the needles you will require. If not, buy them now, as it will save a lot of frustration when you get home.

Substituting yarn

It may be that the yarn recommended for the pattern you want to knit is not available in your favorite color, or that you dislike a particular fiber, and so you may want to change the yarn. While this is possible to do, there are a few points to consider and a calculation to make before you make any change.

The first point to make is that you shouldn't make the decision to change yarns lightly. The pattern designer chose the yarn they used for good reasons, and a different yarn might not produce the same result.

Stitch detail that showed perfectly in a crisp cotton yarn can almost entirely vanish in a fuzzy wool yarn, and a sweater that was soft and cozy in a wool/cashmere yarn might be stiff and uncomfortable in a man-made fiber. A cable pattern originally knitted in cotton will pull in when worked in wool because of the greater elasticity of the yarn and so the fabric will become narrower; this will alter the proportions of the garment.

However, if a yarn substitution is necessary—if there is an allergy to wool, for example—the following is a guideline to making the most informed choices.

Unless you know what you are doing when it comes to altering knitting patterns, you must choose a substitute yarn that is the same weight as the pattern yarn. If you knit a pattern designed for DK yarn in a sport weight yarn, the finished result will be very small indeed unless you make a lot of alterations to the pattern.

Before buying all the yarn needed, buy just one ball and knit a gauge square (page 20) to ensure that you can match the designer's gauge with the substitute yarn: not all yarns made of the same fiber and of the same weight will knit up to the same gauge. The ball band of the substitute yarn will have the manufacturer's gauge printed on it, and as long as that isn't more than one stitch from the designer's gauge, you should be able to get the right gauge by changing needle size.

And you can't just buy the number of balls of yarn asked for in the pattern, as the yarn quantity is calculated by yardage, and your substitute yarn may well not have the same number of yards per ball as the pattern yarn. Having said all that, only simple math is needed to work out how much substitute yarn to buy.

The math is in two parts. Firstly you need to work out the number of yards of yarn in one ball of pattern yarn, multiplied by the number of balls needed, to give you the total yardage of yarn needed.

Then you divide the total yardage needed by the number of yards of yarn in one ball of the substitute yarn to give you the number of balls of substitute yarn you need to buy.

For example:

There are 117 yards per ball of the pattern yarn, and 16 balls are needed.

117 x 16 = 1872 yards of yarn needed.

There are 103 yards per ball of the substitute yarn:
1872 ÷ 103 = 18.17.

So you will need to buy 19 balls of the substitute yarn.

If the sum works out to even a tiny amount over a whole number, you must always round up to the next whole number. And it's a good idea to buy an extra ball, just in case.

GARMENT CARE

Knowing how to care for your hand-knits is important because you want them to look good for as long as possible. Correct washing is particularly essential for baby garments as they need to be washed often.

Check the yarn ball band for washing instructions to see whether the yarn is hand- or machine-washable, and if it is the latter, at what temperature it should be washed.

Most hand-knits should be dried flat on an absorbent cloth, such as a towel, to soak up any moisture. Laying them flat in this way gives you an opportunity to pat the garment back into shape if it has become pulled around in the washing machine. Even if you are in a hurry, do not be tempted to dry your knits near a direct heat source, such as a radiator.

As baby garments are small, you may prefer to hand wash them. Use a washing detergent that is specifically designed for knitwear as this will be kinder to the fabric. Use warm rather than hot water and handle the garment gently without rubbing or wringing. Let the water out of the wash basin and then gently squeeze out the excess water. Do not lift out a water-logged knit as the weight of the water will pull it out of shape. You may need to remove more moisture by rolling it in a towel. Dry flat as above.

EQUIPMENT

There are so many knitting products on the market now that it can be confusing as to what are the essentials and what is just attractive packaging. For the designs in this book, the following is a list of the basic equipment that you will need.

Knitting needles

There is a huge variety of knitting needles to choose from, but the types used in this book are straight and circular. The preference for a type and material is personal to every knitter, but some types may be better suited to different projects; you may prefer a needle with a sharper point with a particular yarn, or shorter needles for knitting small projects. If you have friends who knit, it can be worthwhile borrowing different needles and trying them out with different yarns before deciding what to buy.

Straight knitting needles

Knitting needles are available in different materials; steel, aluminum, wood, bamboo, and plastic, and the choice is down to personal preference. Wood and bamboo needles are good if you are a beginner as they are less slippery than metal or plastic and so the stitches won't slide off them easily.

Needles are sized by thickness according to the US system. The UK and Australia use their own systems of needle sizing. A needle size gauge is inexpensive to buy and is useful if you are using needles marked in a system you are not familiar with, or if the sizing numbers have rubbed off the needle.

As well as thickness sizing, knitting needles come in different lengths, and while it won't make a difference to the knitting, you'll find it easier to handle needles that aren't too long or too short for the number of stitches you have cast on.

Circular needles

These are nylon or plastic cables with a short straight needle at each end. They are used for working larger projects in the round. Circular needles come in different lengths as well as different needle sizes and it's important to use the right length for your projects. You can also work backward and forward on circular needles as you would on straight needles, which is useful for very large projects such as throws or afghans. Using them is also a neat and easy way to knit when traveling.

A circular needle can be fixed, with the needle fused to each end of the cable, or interchangeable, so the needles can be unscrewed and attached to different-length cables. The latter are very versatile, but part of the success with a circular needle depends on the join between needle and cable being very smooth, and with interchangeable needles it may not be.

Cable needles

These short needles are used for working cables and they come in different sizes and styles. Always use a cable needle that is a similar thickness to the knitting needles you are using. A cranked needle or U-shaped cable is a good choice for beginners to cabling, as it makes it almost impossible to drop the stitches that are being moved.

Stitch holders

These are used to keep some stitches separate from others that are being worked on. A safety pin is ideal to hold two or three stitches, but a larger holder will be needed for more stitches. A double-ended stitch holder allows you to knit straight off either end of it. If you need to hold a lot of stitches and don't want a big holder getting in the way, you can thread the stitches onto a strand of yarn. Remember to tie the ends of the strand of yarn firmly together to stop the stitches slipping off it.

Row counter

This little gadget threads onto your knitting needle and you turn the dial every time you complete a row to keep track of how many rows you have completed.

Pins

For finishing and making up projects you will need pins: the types with glass or metal heads are best as they are easy to see and will withstand the heat of the iron. For pinning knitted pieces together before sewing them up, use curved safety pins or seam clips, which won't distort the length of an edge, or stab you while you sew.

Sewing needles

When sewing up seams, use a blunt-tipped tapestry or knitter's sewing needle so that you sew between the knitted stitches without piercing the yarn. A sewing needle with a bent tip is useful for mattress stitch as it makes it easy to see the tip when you push it up between the stitches.

Buttons

Always try to use good-quality buttons that go with the project; I tend to like wooden or "football" type buttons for a more rustic style, and mother-of-pearl for a delicate baby cardigan.

Make sure the buttons are the correct size for the buttonhole; too large will stretch the stitches and too small will be annoying as they will constantly be coming undone. If need be, take the knitted piece with you when buying your buttons.

READING PATTERNS

Some aspects of knitting patterns will vary depending on the style of the designer, manufacturer, or publisher, but there is a common language that runs through them all, and you can expect to find the same basic elements. I'm using the way I set out patterns as examples here, but always check abbreviations and terms in a pattern that's new to you in case details vary. As a novice knitter, decoding pattern language can take some time initially, but once you understand the terminology, you will be able to work from patterns with confidence.

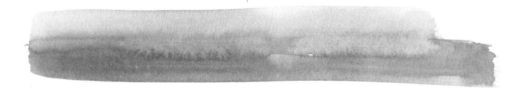

Before you start
Make sure that you have everything you are going to need to complete the pattern. There is little that is more annoying than not being able to complete a project because you didn't buy the specified amount of yarn, and now the dye lot is no longer available.

Do read the pattern through before you start, but don't worry if some of it is unclear; often instructions only make sense once you start knitting them. It's a good idea to mark sizes and measurements needed on the pattern before you start knitting it (see right). And when you pause in your knitting, always mark where you are in the pattern as it can be easy to get confused, especially if you stop for a while.

Sizes and measurements
If a project can be made in different sizes, then the smallest size is printed first and the other sizes follow in brackets, a colon separating each size—for example, "size 0–3(3–6:6–9) months." The same format is used to give instructions for each size—for example, "knit 4(6:8) sts." So, if you were knitting the 3–6 month size, you would knit six stitches for that instruction. It is a good idea to go through a sized pattern and mark the size/instruction you are going to knit in every instance, just so you don't make a mistake. It's even better if you photocopy the pattern and mark the copy; if you knit the garment again in another size you won't get confused.

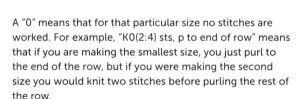

A "0" means that for that particular size no stitches are worked. For example, "K0(2:4) sts, p to end of row" means that if you are making the smallest size, you just purl to the end of the row, but if you were making the second size you would knit two stitches before purling the rest of the row.

The pattern will give some measurements—such as chest and sleeve length—so you should measure the baby before deciding which size to knit. Remember that if you alter the given dimensions—maybe make the garment longer—this will alter the amount of yarn you will need.

If a pattern says "To fit chest…," then the actual garment measurements given are not the same as the measurements of the body size it is designed for. A deliberately baggy sweater might be a couple of inches larger around the chest than the actual chest measurement it is designed to fit. You can get an idea of how loose a fit will be by measuring other baby garments you own before deciding which size to knit.

When both imperial and metric measurements are given, stick to one system throughout, and be careful not to mix the two systems up when working an instruction. Again, marking the measurements you are going to need on the pattern before you start knitting is a good idea.

Materials

The list of materials needed will include the amount of yarn, sizes of needles, and any notions such as buttons or zips. The yarn quantities quoted are based on the gauge instruction (page 20).

Abbreviations

Knitting instructions are usually given in patterns as abbreviations to save space. In this book each new abbreviation is listed on the project page when it's used for the first time, and all of them are listed here. Figures given in italics at the end of a row instruction are the number of stitches that should be on the needle when that row is completed.

Note that not all knitting designers use exactly the same abbreviations, so do check that you understand everything written in a pattern before you start using it.

beg	begin(s)(ning)
C2B	cable two stitches back
C2F	cable two stitches front
C4B	cable four stitches back
C4F	cable four stitches front
C6B	cable six stitches back
C6F	cable six stitches front
cont	continue
dec(s)	decrease(s)(ing)
DK	double knit
foll(s)	follow(s)(ing)
g	gram
in	inch(es)
inc	increase(s)(ing)
k	knit
k2tog	knit two stitches (or number stated) together
k2tog tbl	knit two stitches together through the back loops
m1	make one stitch
m1pw	make one stitch purlwise
mm	millimeter(s)
p	purl
p2tog	purl two stitches (or number stated) together
p2tog tbl	purl two stitches together through the back loops
patt(s)	pattern(s)
psso	pass slipped stitch over
rem	remain(ing)
rep	repeat
skpo	slip one stitch, knit one stitch, pass slipped stitch over
sl	slip
st st	stockinette stitch
st(s)	stitch(es)
yf	yarn forward
yon	yarn over needle
yrn	yarn round needle
[ ]	work instructions within brackets as many times as stated
*	work instructions following/between (single or double) asterisks as many times as stated

GAUGE

Many knitters are guilty of ignoring a pattern's gauge instruction in their eagerness to get started on the project, but when they complete all the (weeks of) knitting and sew up the garment, they discover that it is too big, or too small, even though they followed the pattern exactly. The answer will almost always be that they didn't knit to the correct gauge. It only takes a short time to knit a gauge square; certainly much, much less time than it does to reknit an entire project…

In the instructions for a pattern there will be a gauge instruction; it will usually say something like, "22 sts and 28 rows to 4in over st st using size US 6 needles." What this means is that there must be 22 stitches in a horizontally measured 4in square of your knitted fabric, and 28 rows when you measure it vertically. The point of knitting a gauge square is to make sure that you can get the right number of stitches and rows to the specified measurement.

The ball band of a yarn will have a gauge printed on it, and this is the manufacturer's gauge. But the designer of the pattern you are going to knit may have worked to a different gauge, and it is the designer's gauge that you need to match.

Knitting a gauge square

Using the needles, yarn, and stitch pattern specified in the gauge instruction, cast on at least 10 more stitches than you need to be able to measure; so if the instruction asks for 22 sts to 4in, then cast on at least 32 sts. Work 10 rows more than you need to measure and bind off loosely. Smooth out the square on a flat surface, but do not stretch it. If possible, leave the square to "relax" for a while. You need two pins and a ruler to measure your gauge. Do not use a cloth tape measure as it may not lie completely flat on the square.

To check stitch gauge, lay the ruler horizontally on the square, with the end a few stitches in from an edge. Put in a pin at the end of the ruler and another at the 4in mark. Count the number of stitches between the pins.

To check row gauge, lay the ruler vertically on the square, with the end a few rows down from the bound-off edge. Put in a pin at the end of the ruler and another at the 4in mark. Count the number of rows between the pins.

If the gauge instruction says 22 sts to 4in and you have 23 sts, then you may well be tempted to think that just one stitch difference won't matter. However, when you cast on 110 sts for the brim of a beret, knit the piece, and expect it to measure 19¾in across, yours will measure a shade under 19in. Likewise, if you only have 21 sts to 4in, your 110 sts will measure a tiny amount over 20½in. If the beret is supposed to fit snugly, the difference of ¾in would make it either uncomfortably tight, or loose enough to slip down over your eyes.

If the piece you were knitting was the back of a fitted sweater and you had a similar discrepancy in the front piece, then the whole sweater would be 1½in too small, or 1½in too large. And that is the result of just a single stitch difference from the stated pattern gauge.

The other reason for obtaining accurate gauge is that it will affect how much yarn you use. If you are knitting your project too big, then you will use more yarn than the designer did.

Some projects, such as bags or toys, might say that a specific gauge is not needed for this project. However, it's still a good idea to knit a square, just to see how the yarn looks when knitted to your natural gauge (see right). If, for example, you knit very loosely and you're knitting a bear, then his stuffing might show through the stitches when he's finished.

Changing your gauge

Everyone has a "natural" gauge that they knit to. Some people knit very tightly, others loosely. The way in which you wind the yarn around your fingers, the yarn you are using, and even the material your knitting needles are made from can affect your gauge. Many beginner knitters take a while to settle down to a natural gauge, and if you learn a better way to hold the yarn or needles, your gauge can change.

If you have knitted a gauge square and you do not have the correct number of stitches and rows, then you need to try again. However, you must not try to just knit a bit tighter or looser than your natural gauge; you won't be able to maintain the false gauge, and at best your knitting will be uneven.

What you must do is change the size of the needles you are knitting with. The rule of thumb is that needles one size different will make a difference of one stitch in your gauge. So, if you were using size US 6 needles and needed 22 stitches but had 23, then your gauge is too tight and you need to try again using size US 7 needles. If you only had 19 stitches to 4in, then your gauge is too loose and you should try size US 5 needles.

If you have managed to get the right stitch gauge, but your row gauge is still out by one row, then you can simply work fewer rows. So if the gauge was supposed to be 28 but you had 29, then you can work 27 rows for every 28 given in the pattern, although this can quickly become complicated if stitch patterns, color knitting, or a lot of shaping are involved. However, many simpler garment patterns will tell you to knit pieces to a specified measurement rather than a row count, so if your row gauge is off by one row, it shouldn't make any difference to the look of the finished project.

FIRST STEPS

If you are completely new to knitting, then start by familiarizing yourself with holding the yarn and needles.

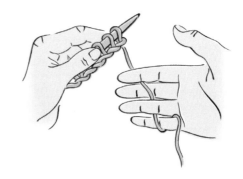

2 Wind the yarn right around your pinky finger, under your third finger, over your center finger, and under your index finger. Use your index finger to wrap the yarn around the tip of the needle. Of the three arrangements shown here, this one puts the most amount of tension on the yarn.

Holding the yarn: US (UK)

For neat knitting, it is important to control the flow of the yarn to the needles in a smooth way that is neither too tight nor too loose. There is no right or wrong way to do this; it is the end result that matters. Hold the yarn in your right hand and, looking at the palm of your hand, wind the yarn around your fingers in one of these three ways.

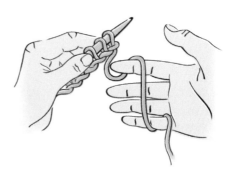

3 Wind the yarn right around your pinky finger, over your third and center fingers, and around your index finger. Use your index finger to wrap the yarn around the tip of the needle. This is the way I hold the yarn.

1 Wind the yarn over your pinky finger, under your third finger, over your center finger, and under your index finger. Use your index finger to wrap the yarn around the tip of the needle. Of the three arrangements shown here, this one puts the least amount of tension on the yarn.

Holding the needles: US (UK)

Knitters tend to hold the needles the way they were taught when they first learned to knit, but it can be useful to try another way to see if it improves your speed or neatness. I hold my needles like a pencil, but if I am working on a large project with many stitches on the needles, I sometimes change to the knife position just to vary the position of my fingers and loosen them up.

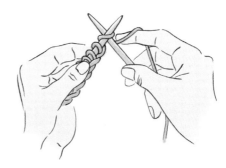

Like a knife

Hold the right-hand needle from above, in the same way as a knife. This method tends to mean you have to let go of the right needle to wrap the yarn around the tip of it, so knitting will be slower than if you hold the needle like a pencil. The right index finger is going to control the tension of the yarn, so it is important to keep the yarn slightly taut around this finger.

The left-hand needle (the one with the stitches on at the start of a row), is held from above, using your thumb and index finger to control the tip of the needle.

Once you are comfortable with holding both the yarn and needles, move on to learning the first knitting techniques. Casting on and US (UK) knit stitch are shown on pages 34–35.

An alternative technique is the Continental method of holding yarn and making stitches, shown on pages 24–26.

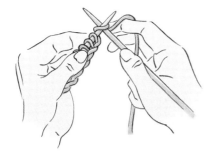

Like a pencil

Hold the right-hand needle in the crook of your thumb, in the same way as a pencil. When casting on and working the first few rows, the knitted fabric will pass over your hand, between your thumb and index finger. As the work grows, slide your thumb under the knitted fabric and hold the needle from below. The right index finger is going to control the tension of the yarn, so it is important to keep the yarn slightly taut around this finger.

The left-hand needle (the one with the stitches on at the start of a row), is held from above, using your thumb and index finger to control the tip of the needle.

Continental method

This way of holding the yarn and needles and forming the stitches is mainly used in Continental Europe, though it is also popular in the US. Some left-handed people find this an easier method than the US (UK) method (page 22).

Holding yarn

Hold the yarn in your left hand and wind it around your fingers in one of the following ways.

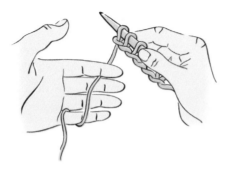

1 Wind the yarn around your pinky finger, over your third finger and center fingers, and under your index finger.

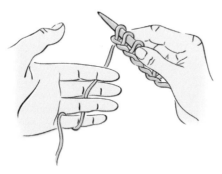

2 Wind the yarn around your pinky finger, under your third finger, over your center finger, and under your index finger. You can also just pass the yarn over your little finger, rather than wrapping around it, if you need less tension.

Holding needles

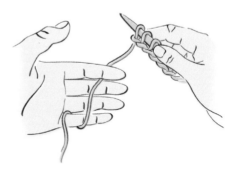

1 Holding the needle with the stitches on in your right hand, wrap the yarn around the fingers of your left hand in the arrangement you prefer.

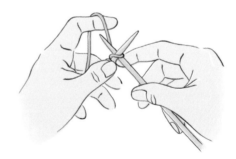

2 Then move the needle with the stitches on into your left hand. The left index finger is going to control the tension of the yarn, so it is important to keep the yarn slightly taut around this finger. Hold the empty right-hand needle from above, gripping it between your thumb and center finger. The right-hand needle can then be inserted into the first stitch on the left-hand needle when you are ready to start knitting.

Knit stitch: Continental

In this method the left hand holds the working yarn instead of the right. Once this technique is mastered, it can be a quick way to knit, but can create a slightly uneven fabric. Knitters who use this method are sometimes called "pickers" because of the way the right-hand needle catches or "picks" the yarn.

1 Hold the yarn and needles the Continental way (see opposite). * With the yarn at the back, from left to right put the tip of the right-hand needle into the first stitch on the left-hand needle.

2 Wrap the working yarn over the tip of the right-hand needle.

3 Lower your left-hand index finger slightly and, keeping the yarn taut over the right-hand needle, draw it, and the yarn wrapped around it, completely through the stitch on the left-hand needle, so forming a new stitch on the right-hand needle.

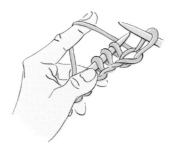

4 Slip the original stitch off the left-hand needle, keeping the new stitch on the right-hand needle. You have knitted one stitch. Repeat from * until all the stitches have been knitted off the left-hand needle onto the right-hand needle: you have knitted one row. Swap the needle with the stitches on into your left hand to start the next row.

Purl stitch: Continental

The purl stitch can be trickier to come to grips with using the Continental method as you are taking the yarn counterclockwise, which can be a bit fiddly. However when alternating knit and purl stitches—as for rib or seed stitch—the Continental method can be the quickest way to create the fabric.

1 Hold the yarn and needles the Continental way (page 24). * With the yarn in front, from right to left put the tip of the right-hand needle into the first stitch on the left-hand needle.

2 Wrap the working yarn over the tip of the right-hand needle, and press the yarn down with the index finger of your left hand to keep it taut.

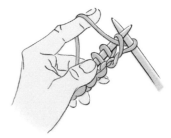

3 Draw the tip of the right-hand needle and the yarn wrapped around it backward through the stitch on the left-hand needle, so forming a new stitch on the right-hand needle.

4 Slip the original stitch off the left-hand needle, keeping the new stitch on the right-hand needle. You have purled one stitch. Repeat from * until all the stitches have been purled off the left-hand needle onto the right-hand needle: you have purled one row. Swap the needle with the stitches on into your left hand to start the next row.

THE
PROJECTS

FIRST

BLANKET

The knit stitch is the first stitch you will learn as you start to knit. It produces a pattern called garter stitch and is used to work this four-color blanket, which is knitted in two strips and sewn together down the center. I have chosen soft pastels, but you may want to use brighter shades, or decorate it with pom-poms or tassels at the corners.

Measurements
19¾ x 27½in

Materials
2 x 1¾oz (50g) balls of Debbie Bliss
Cashmerino Aran in each of
Baby Pink 603 (A), Lime 502 (B),
Beige 102 (C) and Silver 202 (D),
Pair of size US 7 knitting needles

Gauge
20 sts and 38 rows to 4in square
over garter st using size US 7
needles

Abbreviations
A, B, C, D yarn colors as listed
in materials
cont continue
g gram
in inch; inches
k knit (page 35)
st(s) stitch(es)
Also see page 19

THE PATTERN

First half

With size US 7 needles and A,
cast on 50 sts.
Making a slip knot (page 34)
Thumb cast on (page 34)
Work in garter st (k every row)
until piece measures 13¾in from
cast-on edge.
Knit stitch: US (UK) (page 35)
Garter stitch (page 36)
Cut off A.
Join on B.
Joining in a new color (page 36)
Cont in garter st until piece
measures 27½in from cast-on edge.
Bind off.
Binding off (page 36)

Second half

With size US 7 needles and C,
cast on 50 sts.
Work in garter st (k every row)
until piece measures 13¾in from
cast-on edge.
Cut off C.
Join on D.
Cont in garter st until piece
measures 27½in from cast-on edge.
Bind off.

To make up

Join row ends of first half to row
ends of second half, working
through the edge sts to produce
a flat seam.
Flat seam (page 37)
Weave in all ends.
*Sewing in cast-on and bound-off
ends (page 37)*

THE TECHNIQUES

Making a slip knot

The slip knot, sometimes called a "slip loop," creates the very first stitch of a cast on, and almost all casting on methods begin with this knot. The "tail end" is the loose end of the yarn, and the "ball end" is the end running to the ball.

1 Make a loop as shown, taking the tail end of the yarn over the ball end and then under the loop.

2 Slip a knitting needle under the tail end of the yarn. The tail should be at least 4in, but you can leave a longer tail and use it to sew up a seam.

3 Holding both ends of the yarn in one hand, pull the needle upward to tighten the knot. Cast on stitches as required (see below) and work the first row, then pull gently on the tail of yarn to tighten the knot as needed.

Thumb cast on

Because the thumb method is a looser cast on, it is good when you need some elasticity; for example, when a cuff or brim of a hat is turned back so the fabric is doubled. On garter stitch it creates a very neat edge that looks like the rest of the fabric. The downside can be that you are working toward the end, or tail, of the yarn, so you need to estimate the length needed to cast on all the stitches required: a simple formula is to allow ¾in per stitch.

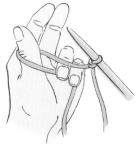

1 Measure out the required length of yarn and make a slip knot (see left). Hold this needle in your right hand. * Wrap the tail end of the yarn around your left thumb from front to back.

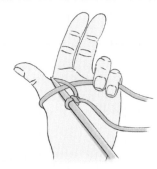

2 Using your right hand, slip the point of a knitting needle under the yarn wrapped around your thumb, as shown.

3 With your right index finger, wrap the ball end of the yarn over the point of the needle.

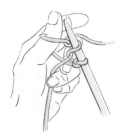

4 Pull the needle, and the loop of yarn around it, under the yarn wrapped around your thumb.

5 Slip your left thumb out of the yarn wrapped around it. Pull gently on the tail end of the yarn to tighten the stitch. Repeat from * until the required number of stitches have been cast on.

Knit stitch: US (UK)

The knit stitch is the easiest to create and the one that beginners will learn first. It is worked from the cast-on row as shown here, and the yarn is always held at the back of the work.

1 Hold the needle with the stitches on in your left hand, with the working yarn at the back, controlled by your right hand (page 22). * Insert the right-hand needle from left to right through the front of the first stitch on the left-hand needle.

2 Wrap the working yarn from left to right over the tip of the right-hand needle.

3 Keeping the yarn taut over the right-hand needle, begin to draw the needle back through the stitch on the left-hand needle.

4 Draw the right-hand needle, and the yarn wrapped over it, completely through the stitch, so forming a stitch on the right-hand needle.

5 Slip the original stitch off the left-hand needle, keeping the new stitch on the right-hand needle. You have knitted one stitch. Repeat from * until all the stitches have been knitted off the left-hand needle onto the right-hand needle: you have knitted one row. Swap the needle with the stitches on into your left hand to start the next row. If you are working garter stitch (page 36) then the next row will be another knit row. If you are working stockinette stitch (page 54), the next row will be a purl row (page 52).

Garter stitch

This is the simplest stitch pattern; you just knit every stitch and every row. Garter stitch is usually what a beginner knitter chooses for their first project, but its neat texture and the stable, flat, reversible fabric it produces make it an essential stitch for master knitters, too.

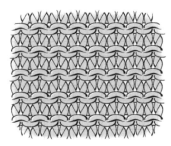

Joining in a new color

When you change yarn colors, always do so at the edge of the knitting, not in the middle of a row.

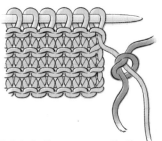

1 To join in the new yarn, tie the free end around the tail (which should be approximately 6in in length) of the old yarn in a single knot.

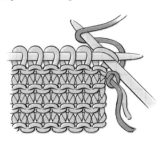

2 Slip the knot up the tail of the old yarn until it is tight against the knitting, then start the row using the new yarn. When you have completed the knitting, you can unpick the knot (if need be) and sew the ends in.

Binding off

This is the most commonly used bind off technique. Be careful not to work it too tightly and so make an edge that isn't at all stretchy.

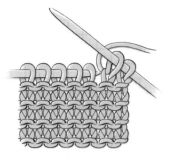

1 Knit the first two stitches on the left-hand needle.

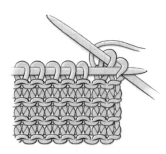

2 * Slip the tip of the left-hand needle through the front of the first stitch on the right-hand needle.

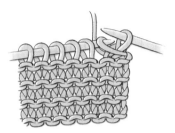

3 Lift this stitch over the second stitch, then drop it off the needle. You have bound off one stitch.

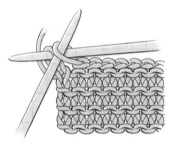

4 Knit the next stitch and repeat from * until all stitches have been worked off the left-hand needle and only one stitch remains on the right-hand needle.

5 Leaving a 6in tail to weave in later (see right), or sew a seam with (see right), cut the yarn. Slip the last stitch off the needle and pass the end of the yarn through it. Pull on the tail to pull the stitch tight and so fasten off.

Flat seam

This seam is particularly good for babies as there is no bulky edge to rub against skin. However, it is not a very strong seam and the stitches can stretch. It is worked on the wrong side.

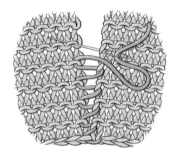

1 Wrong sides up, lay the two edges to be joined side by side. Thread a blunt-tipped sewing needle with a long length of yarn and secure the yarn on the back of one piece. Take the needle under the bump of the first edge stitch on one side, then under the corresponding bump on the edge of the other piece. Continue in this way, zigzagging between the stitch bumps, as shown, and pulling the seam gently tight as you work.

Sewing in cast-on and bound-off ends

When casting on and binding off, leave the yarn tails as long as possible and use them to sew up the seams. But if an edge is not being seamed, then sew the tail tidily into the back of the knitting

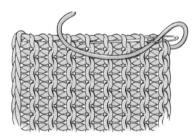

1 If the edge is not going to be taken into a seam, then thread the end of the tail into a blunt-tipped sewing needle. Take the needle under a few stitches along the edge of the knitting then, skipping the last stitch, take it back through the stitches. If the yarn is thick, then go through the stitches in one direction only. Trim the end close to the knitting. The principle is the same whatever the knitting stitch pattern is.

If the edge is going to be taken into a seam, but you are not going to use the end to sew up with, then sew the seam first. Then use the method above to sew the end into the edge that was taken into the seam.

BEANIE

I find it very soothing to knit a beanie and the babies of family and friends always get one gifted from me. A small project like this is portable, too, for knitting on the run. Worked in easy garter stitch, this hat will introduce you to decreasing to shape the crown.

Measurements
To fit ages
3–6   6–12   months
Pattern note: Sizes (page 40)

Materials
1(2) x 1¾oz (50g) balls of Debbie Bliss Baby Cashmerino in Tobacco
Pair of size US 3 knitting needles

Gauge
25 sts and 50 rows to 4in square over garter st using size US 3 needles

Abbreviations
foll(s)   follow(s)(ing)
k2tog   knit two stitches (or number stated) together (page 40)
[]   work instructions within square brackets as many times as stated
Also see page 19

Note
Figures given in italics at the end of a row instruction are the number of stitches that should be on the needle when that row is complete.

THE PATTERN

Hat

With size US 3 needles, cast on
91(101) sts.
Work in garter st (k every row)
throughout until piece measures
5½(6¼)in from cast-on edge.
Shape top
Cont in garter st, shaping as folls:
Next row: K1, [k2tog, k8] 9(10) times.
82(91) sts
Knit two together (see right)
Work 3 rows without shaping.
Next row: K1, [k2tog, k7] 9(10) times.
73(81) sts
Work 3 rows without shaping.
Next row: K1, [k2tog, k6] 9(10) times.
64(71) sts
Work 3 rows without shaping.
Next row: K1, [k2tog, k5] 9(10) times.
55(61) sts
Work 3 rows without shaping.
Next row: K1, [k2tog, k4] 9(10) times.
46(51) sts
Work 1 row without shaping.
Next row: K1, [k2tog, k3] 9(10) times.
37(41) sts
Work 1 row without shaping.
Next row: K1, [k2tog, k2] 9(10) times.
28(31) sts
Work 1 row without shaping.
Next row: K1, [k2tog, k1] 9(10) times.
19(21) sts
Next row: K1, [k2tog] to end.
10(11) sts
Break yarn, leaving a long end,
thread the end through rem sts, pull
up and secure.

To make up

Join the back seam, working through
the edge sts to produce a flat seam.
Weave in all ends.
Fold back the edge to form a
folded brim.

THE TECHNIQUES

Knit two together

This is the easiest decrease to work
as it simply involves knitting two
stitches together as one. It is usually
abbreviated to "k2tog."

1 Insert the right-hand needle
knitwise through the next two
stitches on the left-hand needle
instead of through one.

2 Wind the yarn around the tip of
the right-hand needle and draw a
loop through both stitches.

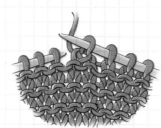

3 Drop both stitches together off
the left-hand needle. You have
decreased by one stitch.

Pattern note: Sizes

If a project can be made in different
sizes, then within the pattern
instructions the smallest size is
printed first and the other sizes
follow in brackets, a colon
separating each size—for example,
"size 8(10:12)." The same format is
used to give instructions for each
size—for example, "K4(6:8) sts." So
if you were knitting the largest size,
you would knit 8 stitches for that
instruction. It is a good idea to go
through a sized pattern and mark
the size/instruction you are going
to knit in every instance, just so
you don't make a mistake. It's even
better if you photocopy the pattern
and mark the copy; if you knit the
garment again in another size you
won't get confused.

A "0" means that for that particular
size no stitches are worked. For
example, "K0(2:4) sts, p to end of
row" means that if you are making
the smallest size, you just purl to
the end of the row, but if you were
making the second size you would
knit two stitches before purling the
rest of the row.

CARRY
BAG

A carry bag is a great modern alternative to a wrap-around shawl: just pop baby in and let them snuggle down into it. Knitted in garter stitch, this design has a button fastening so now you can learn how to work buttonholes.

Measurements

To fit ages

0–3	3–6	months

Length to top of head

27½	29½	in

Materials

7(8) x 1¾oz (50g) balls of Debbie Bliss Cashmerino Aran in Beige 102
Pair of size US 7 knitting needles
6 buttons

Gauge

20 sts and 38 rows to 4in square over garter st using size US 7 needles

Abbreviations

rep	repeat
yf	yarn forward
**	work instructions following/between asterisks as many times as stated

Also see page 19

Note

The first and last 10 sts of the back will be folded to form part of the front.

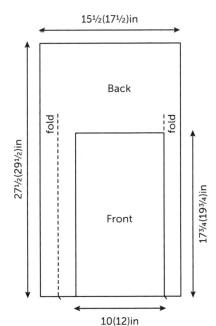

15½(17½)in

Back

27½(29½)in

fold

fold

17¾(19¾)in

Front

10(12)in

THE PATTERN

Back

With size US 7 needles, cast on
80(90) sts.
K 266(286) rows, ending with a right
side row.
Bind off.
Place a marker 10 sts in from each
end of the cast-on edge.
*Pattern note: Placing markers
(page 46)*

Front

With size US 7 needles, cast on
50(60) sts.
K 25(45) rows, ending with a wrong
side row.
** Buttonhole row: K2, k2tog, yf,
k to end.
Eyelet buttonhole (page 46)
K 27 rows **.
Rep from ** to ** 4 times more.
Buttonhole row: K2, k2tog, yf,
k to end.
K 7 rows.
Bind off.

To make up

Join the non-buttonhole edge of
the front to the edge of the back,
working into row-end sts to create
a flat seam.
Fold the sides of the back onto the
front at the cast-on edge markers.
Leaving 10 sts at the right-hand side
free for the button band, join the
cast-on edges together matching
right-hand side of the front to the
marker. Sew the 10 cast-on sts of
the button band to the wrong side
of the front.
*Mattress stitch on garter stitch:
joining cast-on and bound-off edges
(page 46)*
Weave in all ends.
Sew on buttons.
*Pattern note: Sewing on buttons
(page 47)*
Fold bound-off edge of the back
in half and join to form the top of
the hood.

THE TECHNIQUES

Pattern note: Placing markers

You can use short lengths of a contrasting color yarn, small safety pins, or purchased stitch markers. The pattern will tell you where to place the marker on the work.

For the carry bag it says: "Place a marker 10 sts in from each end of the cast-on edge." So you need to count along the cast-on edge for 10 sts on the left- and right-hand sides, then place the marker between the 10th and 11th sts. If you use yarn markers, thread the contrast yarn onto a sewing-up needle and just insert the needle between the sts and tie the 2 ends of the yarn.

On garments, it might say: "Place a marker at each end of last row," in which case you add the marker in the same way, but on the edge st at each end of the row.

Eyelet buttonhole

This is the smallest buttonhole you can make, so it is particularly good for items such as baby clothes. It also works well with chunkier yarns where other methods would produce too big a buttonhole. This is also the way to make eyelets for threading cord or ribbon through. It's shown here on garter stitch, but it can be worked in any stitch pattern.

1 On a knit row, work to the position of the buttonhole. Bring the yarn forward between the needles ready to make a yarnover (page 72).

2 Make the yarnover and knit the next two stitches together (page 40) to maintain the original stitch count.

Mattress stitch on garter stitch: joining cast-on and bound-off edges

Mattress stitch is extremely neat, and it is my preferred method for almost every type of seaming. As it is worked from the right side, you can see exactly what you are doing as you sew along the seam.

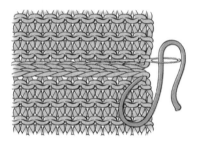

1 Right sides up, lay the two pieces to be joined edge to edge. Thread a blunt-tipped sewing needle with a long length of yarn. Secure the yarn on the back of the lower knitted piece, then bring the needle up through the middle of the first whole stitch in that piece. Take the needle under both loops of the first whole stitch on the upper piece, so that it emerges between the first and second stitches.

2 * Go back into the lower piece and take the needle through to the back where it first came out, and then bring it back to the front in the middle of the next stitch along. Pull the yarn through.

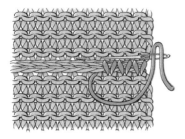

3 Take the needle under both loops of the next whole stitch on the upper piece. Repeat from * to sew the seam, gently pulling the sewn stitches taut.

Pattern note: Sewing on buttons

When sewing buttons onto a child's garment, always make sure that they are bound on really firmly: a loose button can easily find its way into a small mouth.

Unless it is a fancy yarn, use the same yarn as the garment—you can always split the yarn if you need a thinner strand for sewing on.

PANTS

These pants are perfect to encase plump baby legs. They are knitted in stockinette stitch, which is a combination of the knit stitch and the purl stitch that you are going to learn how to work now. Wide elastic sewn at the waist makes the pants fit snugly without being too tight.

Measurements

To fit ages

0–3	3–6	6–9	9–12	months

Finished measurements

16¼	18	20	22	in

Length

13	14½	16¼	18	in

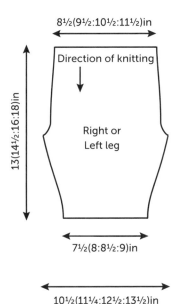

8½(9½:10½:11½)in

Direction of knitting

Right or Left leg

13(14½:16:18)in

7½(8:8½:9)in

10½(11¼:12½:13½)in

Materials

2(2:3:3) x 1¾oz (50g) balls of Debbie Bliss Baby Cashmerino in Wasabi 313
Pair each of size US 2–3 and size US 3 knitting needles
Waist length of ½in wide elastic

Gauge

25 sts and 34 rows to 4in square over st st using size US 3 needles

Abbreviations

beg	begin(s)(ning)
dec(s)	decrease(s)(ing)
inc	increase(s)(ing)
m1	make one stitch (page 53)
p	purl (page 52)
skpo	slip one, knit one, pass slipped stitch over (page 54)

Also see page 19

Note from the author: I write my patterns using UK sizes for needles and make the necessary conversions for my readers in the US. Occasionally, this can be problematic. The ribbing for these pants is written using metric size 3mm needles for which there is no US equivalent—it falls somewhere between sizes 2 and US 3. Your local yarn store may stock 3mm needles, or look for them online. Alternatively, use either size US 2 or 3.

THE PATTERN

Legs (Make 2)

With size US 2 or 3 needles, cast on 54(60:66:72) sts.

Rib row: [K1, p1] to end.

Purl stitch: US (UK) (page 52)

This row **forms** the rib and is repeated 9 times more.

Single rib (page 52)

Change to size US 3 needles.

Pattern note: Changing needle sizes (page 53)

Beg with a k row, work in st st until work measures 5½(6¼:6¾:7½)in from cast-on edge, ending with a p row.

Stockinette stitch (page 54)

Shape crotch

Inc row: K1, m1, k to last st, m1, k1.

Make one stitch (page 53)

P 1 row.

Rep the last 2 rows 1(1:2:2) times more, then rep the inc row again. 60(66:74:80) sts

P 1 row.

Cast on 3 sts at beg of next 2 rows. 66(72:80:86) sts

Shape for legs

Work 2 rows.

Dec row: K2, skpo, k to last 4 sts, k2tog, k2.

Slip one, knit one, pass slipped stitch over (page 54)

Knit two together (page 54)

Pattern note: Fully fashioned shaping (page 55)

P 1 row.

Rep the last 2 rows 2(3:4:5) times. 60(64:70:74) sts

Dec row: K2, skpo, k to last 4 sts, k2tog, k2.

Work 5 rows.

Rep the last 6 rows 4(5:6:7) times and the dec row again. 48(50:54:56) sts

Work 7(7:9:11) rows.

Change to size US 2 or 3 needles.

Rib row: [K1, p1] to end.

This row forms the rib and is repeated 9 times more.

Bind off in rib.

Binding off in pattern (page 55)

To make up

Join inner leg seams using mattress stitch, working the correct version for each stitch pattern.

Mattress stitch on stockinette stitch: joining row ends to row ends (page 56)

Mattress stitch on single rib: joining row ends to row ends (page 57)

Join center front and back seam using mattress stitch.

Weave in all ends.

Join the elastic into a ring. Work a herringbone casing on the wrong side, over the waist rib, enclosing the elastic.

Stitching in elastic (page 57)

THE TECHNIQUES

Single rib

This stitch has a natural elasticity and is most commonly used for welts and cuffs on garments such as sweaters and cardigans. It is made up of alternate knit and purl stitches across a row, and on subsequent rows the stitches that were purled on the previous row are knitted, and vice versa.

The exact pattern depends on whether the ribbing is being worked over an even or odd number of stitches.

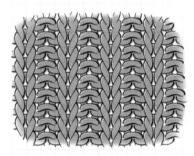

For an even number of stitches
1st row: [K1, p1] to end.
Rep 1st row as required.

For an odd number of stitches
1st row: [K1, p1] to last st, k1.
2nd row: [P1, k1] to last st, p1.
Rep 1st and 2nd rows as required.

Purl stitch: US (UK)

The purl stitch is the other basic stitch to learn and is worked in the opposite way to the knit stitch. Some beginners may find it slightly more difficult to master than the knit stitch, but the principle is still the same. The yarn is always held at the front of the work.

1 Hold the needle with the stitches on in your left hand, with the working yarn at the front, controlled by your right hand (page 22). * Insert the right-hand needle from right to left through the front of the first stitch on the left-hand needle.

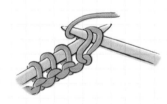

2 Wrap the working yarn from right to left around the tip of the right-hand needle.

3 Keeping the yarn wrapped around the right-hand needle, begin to draw the needle backward through the stitch on the left-hand needle.

4 Draw the right-hand needle, and the yarn wrapped around it, completely through the stitch, so forming a stitch on the right-hand needle.

5 Slip the original stitch off the left-hand needle, keeping the new stitch on the right-hand needle. You have purled one stitch. Repeat from * until all the stitches have been purled off the left-hand needle onto the right-hand needle: you have purled one row. Swap the needle with the stitches on into your left hand to start the next row. If you are working stockinette stitch (page 54), the next row will be a knit row (page 35).

Make one stitch

This method is one of the neatest and creates a virtually invisible increase, so it can be used in the middle of a row. The slight hole it can create is closed by knitting into the back of the raised strand, thus twisting it. It is usually abbreviated as "m1" or "m1l": if a pattern just says "m1," this is the increase it refers to. The increase slopes to the left on stockinette stitch. This increase is also known as a "raised increase."

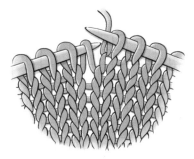

1 From the front, slip the tip of the left-hand needle under the horizontal strand of yarn lying between the last stitch on the right-hand needle and the first stitch on the left-hand needle.

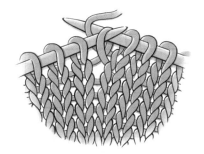

2 Insert the right-hand needle knitwise into the back of the loop formed by the strand.

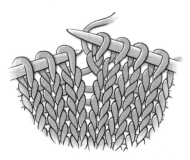

3 Knit the loop in the same way you would knit a stitch through the back loop. You have increased by one stitch.

Pattern note: Changing needle size

To change from one needle size to another you do not need to manually transfer the stitches from the old needles to the new needles, you simply work the next row with a new needle in your right hand, then proceed with both new needles. Changing from one size needle to another is usually done when you want to increase or decrease the width of the fabric. On ribbed hems, cuff, and neckbands it makes a firmer fabric that still keeps its elasticity: on these pants it creates a snug fit at the bottom of the legs and brings the waist in.

Stockinette stitch

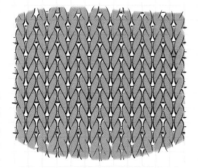

Stockinette stitch is the most popular of all knitted fabrics and is made up of alternate rows of knit and purl stitches. The rows and columns of interlocking V shapes create a smooth surface that is a perfect background for areas of stitch texture, and that shows off the qualities of textural yarns.

Slip one, knit one, pass slipped stitch over

This decrease slants to the left on stockinette stitch. It is similar in appearance to k2tog (see right) and so is good paired with that decrease when working symmetrical, fully fashioned shaping (see opposite). It is abbreviated in knitting patterns as "skpo" or "skp."

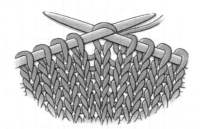

1 Insert the right-hand needle knitwise into the next stitch on the left-hand needle, and slip it onto the right-hand needle.

2 Knit the next stitch in the usual way.

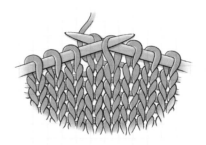

3 Use the left-hand needle to lift the slipped stitch on the right-hand needle over the stitch just knitted, then drop it off both needles. You have decreased by one stitch.

Knit two together

This decrease always involves knitting two stitches together, no matter what the stitch pattern is. It slants to the right on stockinette stitch and so is usually used when working the left side of an edge shaping to slant in the same direction as the fabric. This decrease is abbreviated to "k2tog."

1 Insert the right-hand needle knitwise through the next two stitches on the left-hand needle instead of through one.

2 Wind the yarn around the tip of the right-hand needle and draw a loop through both stitches.

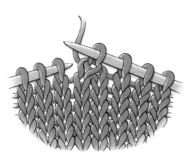

3 Drop both stitches together off the left-hand needle. You have decreased by one stitch.

Binding off in pattern

By binding off in rib you produce a stretchier bound-off edge, which is particularly useful in ensuring that an edge is not too tight. The principle applies to all stitch patterns.

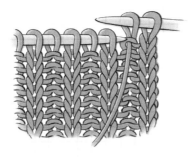

1 Knit one stitch, then purl one stitch, following the rib pattern.

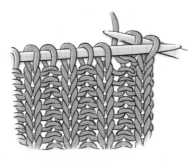

2 Take the yarn to the back, ready to work the next stitch, then use the tip of the left-hand needle to lift the first stitch over the second stitch. Complete the bind off in this way, knitting or purling the stitches following the stitch pattern, then fasten off as for a standard bind off (page 36).

Pattern note: Fully fashioned shaping

With this technique, the increases and decreases are worked two or three stitches in from the edge of the knitting, so they are a visible feature. This creates decorative detailing that can give interest to a plain stockinette stitch garment.

As they are designed to be seen, you need to pair increases and decreases to slope the right way. At the start of a right-side row in stockinette stitch, "skpo" (see opposite) slants to the left, paired with "k2tog" (see opposite), which slants to the right, at the end of the row.

Mattress stitch on stockinette stitch: joining row ends to row ends

You can take a whole stitch in from the edge for neatness as here, or half a stitch if you are working with a fairly thick yarn and don't want the seam to be too bulky. Closing up the seam with half a stitch makes a whole stitch that is not quite symmetrical, so this doesn't create such an invisible join as when taking in a whole stitch.

1 Right sides up, lay the two edges to be joined side by side. Thread a blunt-tipped sewing needle with a long length of yarn. Secure the yarn on the back of the right-hand knitted piece. To start the seam, from the back bring the needle up between the first and second stitches of that piece, immediately above the cast-on edge. Take it across to the left-hand piece, and

from the back bring it through between the first and second stitches of that piece, immediately above the cast-on edge. Take it back to the right-hand piece and, again from the back, bring it through one row above where it first came through, between the first and second stitches. Pull the yarn through and this figure-of-eight will hold the cast-on edges level.

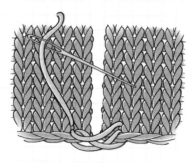

2 Take the needle across to the left-hand piece and, from the front, take it under the bar of yarn above where it last came out on that side, between the first and second stitches.

3 * Take the needle across to the right-hand piece and, from the front, take it under the next two bars of yarn between the first and second stitches. Pull the yarn through. Then take the needle back to the left-hand piece and, from the front, under the corresponding two bars between the first and second stitches.

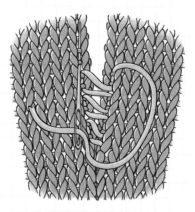

4 Repeat from * to sew the seam. When you have sewn about 1¼in, gently pull the stitches up tight to close the seam, and then continue.

Mattress stitch on single rib: joining row ends to row ends

Both pieces must start and end with the same stitch, which will usually be a knit stitch, as shown here. You will be taking in half a stitch on each side, which when the edges are drawn together will create a whole stitch, thus keeping the rib pattern continuous across the seam.

1 Use the same technique as for sewing stockinette stitch row ends to row ends (see opposite), but take the needle through the center of the first stitch on each knitted piece, instead of between the first and second stitches.

Stitching in elastic

As there is only a single layer of fabric—rather than the double layer of a casing—this method does not introduce extra bulk.

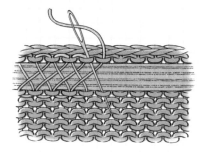

1 Measure the elastic, overlap the ends, making sure the elastic isn't twisted, and sew them firmly together. Pin the loop of elastic in place on the wrong side of the garment, just below the top finished edge. Thread a blunt-tipped sewing needle with a long length of yarn and secure the yarn on the back of the piece above the elastic.
* Working from left to right, take the needle under the loop of the back of a stitch just below the elastic, and then take it up under the stitch loop immediately to the left. Take the needle over the elastic and across to the right making a diagonal stitch, then take it up under the loop of the back of a stitch just above the elastic, and then down under the stitch loop immediately to the left. Make a diagonal stitch down across the elastic to the next stitch loop to the right of the last one with a stitch in below the elastic and repeat from *. Pull the stitches gently taut but not tight.

COWL

A cozy cowl is usually easier to keep on a baby than a scarf and can be tucked into a collar to keep out the chill. Using knit and purl stitches in the same row forms a rib pattern, and by knitting on a circular needle you prevent an unattractive seam.

Measurements
One size to fit ages 6 months– 2 years

Materials
1 x 1¾oz (50g) ball of Debbie Bliss Baby Cashmerino in Light Pink
1 x size US 3 short circular needle

Gauge
25 sts and 34 rows over st st and 45 sts and 34 rows over patt, both to 4in square using size US 3 needles

Abbreviations
See page 19

THE PATTERN

Cowl

With size US 3 circular needle, cast on 114 sts, taking care not to twist sts.

Knitting in the round on a circular needle (see right)

Place a stitch marker between first and last cast on sts to indicate beg and end of rounds.

Join to make a round and work as follows:

Every round: [K3, p3] to the end of round, slip marker.

This round forms 3 x 3 rib and is repeated a further 48 times.

(49 rounds worked in total)

Remove the marker and bind off in rib.

To make up

Weave in the cast-on and bound-off tails of yarn to neaten the edges between the beg and end of the round.

THE TECHNIQUES

Knitting in the round on a circular needle

A circular needle is two short knitting needles connected by a flexible cable. It is important to have the right length needle for the number of stitches; too short and the stitches will fall off or be bunched, too long and the stitches will be stretched.

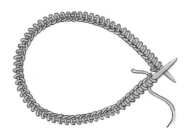

1 Cast on to one of the points of the needle the number of stitches needed; just ignore the cable connecting the two points and cast on the stitches as if you were using two separate needles. Spread out the cast-on stitches along the length of the cable; they should fill it between the two points without being stretched.

2 The first stitch in the first round is the beginning of the round, and all subsequent rounds start in the same position unless the pattern instructs otherwise. To keep track of the rounds, place a round marker on the needle at the start of the first round, before knitting the first stitch.

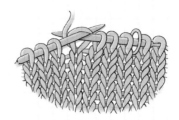

3 Simply knit the stitches from the right-hand point of the needle to the left-hand point, sliding them around the cable as you work. When you get back to the marker, you have completed one round. Slip the marker onto the right-hand point of the needle and knit the next round. All rounds are knitted from the right side of the fabric.

RAGLAN
SWEATER

A very simple sweater in stockinette stitch with raglan sleeves. The gently rolled hems at the neck, sleeves, and body makes it easier to slip the sweater over a baby's head, diaper, and chubby wrists, as there are no tight ribs to contend with.

Measurements

To fit ages

0–3	3–6	6–9	9–12	12–18	18–24	months

Finished measurements

Chest

19¾	20¾	22	23½	25¼	27¼	in

Length to shoulder

8¾	10	11	12¼	13½	14½	in

Sleeve length (with rolled cuff)

5½	6¼	7	8	8¾	9½	in

Materials

3(3:4:4:5:5) x 1¾oz (50g balls of Debbie Bliss Cashmerino Aran in Beige 102
Pair of size US 8 knitting needles

Gauge

18 sts and 24 rows to 4in square over st st using size US 8 needles

Abbreviations

See page 19

Back & Front

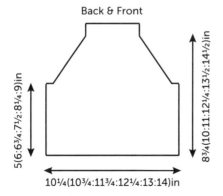

5(6:6¾:7½:8¼:9)in

8¾(10:11:12¼:13½:14½)in

10¼(10¾:11¾:12¼:13:14)in

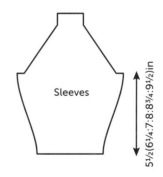

Sleeves

5½(6¼:7:8:8¾:9½)in

THE PATTERN

Back and Front

(Both alike)

With size US 8 needles, cast on 47(50:53:56:60:64) sts.

Cable cast on (see right)

Beg with a k row, work in st st until work measures 5(6:6¾:7½:8¼:9) in from cast-on edge, ending with a p row.

Shape raglans

Bind off 3 sts at beg of next 2 rows. *41(44:47:50:54:58) sts*

1st row: K2, skpo, k to last 4 sts, k2tog, k2.

2nd row: P to end.

Rep the last 2 rows 9(10:11:12:14:15) times. *21(22:23:24:24:26) sts*

Beg with a k row, work 6 rows in st st.

Bind off.

Binding off knitwise (page 66)

Sleeves

(Both alike)

With size US 8 needles, cast on 24(26:28:30:32:34) sts.

Beg with a k row, work 12(14:14:16:16:18) rows in st st.

Inc row: K3, m1, k to last 3 sts, m1, k3.

Beg with a p row, work 3 rows in st st.

Rep the last 4 rows 4(5:6:7:8:9) times more. *34(38:42:46:50:54) sts*

Cont straight until sleeve measures 6¼(7:8:8¾:9½:10¼)in from cast-on edge, ending with a p row.

Shape raglan top

Bind off 3 sts at beg of next 2 rows. *28(32:36:40:44:48) sts*

1st row: K2, skpo, k to last 4 sts, k2tog, k2.

2nd row: P to end.

Rep the last 2 rows 9(10:11:12:14:15) times. *8(10:12:14:14:16) sts*

Beg with a k row, work 6 rows in st st.

Bind off.

To make up

Reversing seam for last 6 rows at neck edge, join raglan seams.

Mattress stitch on stockinette stitch: joining cast-on and bound-off edges (page 67)

Mattress stitch on reverse stockinette stitch: joining row ends to row ends (page 67)

Join side and sleeve seams, reversing seam for last 6 rows at cuff edge.

Weave in all ends.

THE TECHNIQUES

Cable cast on

This cast on uses two needles and follows the same technique as the knit stitch (page 35). It has the advantage of not needing to estimate the amount of yarn needed as you are working using the yarn from the ball. As it is not as elastic as the thumb method (page 34), the cable cast on can be useful in areas where some sturdiness is required, such as the cuff of a sleeve that can get a lot of wear.

1 Make a slip knot about 4in from the end of the yarn. Hold this needle in your left hand. Insert the right-hand needle through the front of the slip knot, below the left-hand needle.

2 Bring the working yarn up and then over the point of the right-hand needle.

3 * Pull the right-hand needle, and the yarn wrapped over it, through the slip knot to make a new loop on the right-hand needle.

4 Place this loop on the left-hand needle, as shown. Gently pull the working yarn to tighten the stitch.

5 Insert the right-hand needle between the slip knot and the first stitch on the left-hand needle. Wrap the yarn over the point of the right-hand needle. Repeat from * until the required number of stitches has been cast on, inserting the needle between the previous two stitches each time.

Binding off knitwise

This is the most commonly used bind off. On a stockinette stitch neckband, be careful not to bind off too tightly.

1 Knit the first two stitches on the left-hand needle.

2 * Slip the tip of the left-hand needle through the front of the first stitch on the right-hand needle.

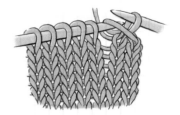

3 Lift this stitch over the second stitch, then drop it off the needle. You have bound off one stitch.

4 Knit the next stitch and repeat from * until all stitches have been worked off the left-hand needle and only one stitch remains on the right-hand needle.

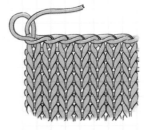

5 Leaving a 6in tail to weave in later, or sew a seam with, cut the yarn. Slip the last stitch off the needle and pass the end of the yarn through it. Pull on the tail to pull the stitch tight and so fasten off.

Mattress stitch on stockinette stitch: joining cast-on and bound-off edges

Mattress stitch matches stitch to stitch and row to row and so it is the most accurate method of joining pieces together, and is virtually invisible. This is how to join cast-on and bound-off edges in stockinette stitch.

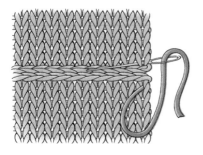

1 Right sides up, lay the two pieces to be joined edge to edge. Thread a blunt-tipped sewing needle with a long length of yarn. Secure the yarn on the back of the lower knitted piece, then bring the needle up through the middle of the first whole stitch in that piece. Take the needle under both loops of the first whole stitch on the upper piece so that it emerges between the first and second stitches.

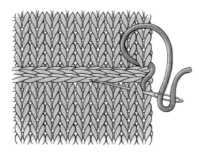

2 * Go back into the lower piece and take the needle through to the back where it first came out, and then bring it back to the front in the middle of the next stitch along. Pull the yarn through.

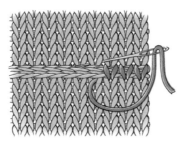

3 Take the needle under both loops of the next whole stitch on the upper piece. Repeat from * to sew the seam. You can either gently pull the sewn stitches taut but have them visible, as shown, so that they continue the stockinette stitch pattern, or you can pull them completely tight so that they disappear.

Mattress stitch on reverse stockinette stitch: joining row ends to row ends

Use this method of mattress stitching if reverse stockinette stitch is used at the edges on the right side of the work, for example in a traditional cable pattern.

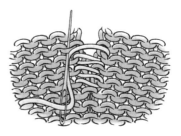

1 Use the same technique as for sewing stockinette stitch row ends to row ends (page 56), but take the needle under only one bar of yarn at a time on each knitted piece for a neat finish.

LACE
BLANKET

The lace stitch on this blanket looks incredibly complex to tackle, but in fact it is one of the easiest patterns to knit. It is formed from repeating just four rows where stitches are decreased and increased to make eyelets in a wave design. The pattern also creates a beautiful scalloped effect on the cast-on edge.

Measurements
23½ x 27½in

Materials
6 x 1¾oz (50g) balls of Debbie Bliss Eco Baby in Ecru 16
Pair of size US 3 needles

Gauge
30 sts and 32 rows to 4in square over patt using 3.25mm size US 3 needles

Abbreviations
p2tog   purl two stitches (or number stated) together (page 70)
patt(s)   pattern(s)
yon   yarnover (page 72)
Also see page 19

THE PATTERN

Blanket

With size US 3 needles, cast
on 152 sts.
K 3 rows.
Now work in patt as follows:
1st row (right side): K to end.
2nd row: K4, p to last 4 sts, k4.
3rd row: K4, *[p2tog] 4 times,
[yon, k1] 8 times, [p2tog] 4 times;
rep from * to last 4 sts, k4.
Purl two together (see right)
Yarnovers (page 72)
4th row: K4, p to last 4 sts, k4.
These 4 rows **form** the patt and
are repeated.
Cont in patt until work measures
26¾in, ending with a 4th patt row.
K 3 rows.
Bind off knitwise on wrong side.

To make up

Weave in all ends.

THE TECHNIQUES

Purl two together

This involves simply purling two
stitches together to make one
stitch. It slants to the right on
stockinette stitch (to the left on
reverse stockinette stitch), so is
usually used on the wrong
side when working the left side
of a shaping such as a neck. It is
usually abbreviated to "p2tog" in
a knitting pattern.

2 Wind the yarn around the tip
of the right-hand needle and draw
a loop through both stitches.

1 Insert the right-hand needle
purlwise through the next two
stitches on the left-hand needle
instead of through one.

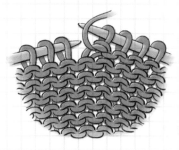

3 Drop both stitches together off
the left-hand needle. You have
decreased by one stitch.

Yarnovers

Lace patterns range from the simple to the more intricate but all are based on making yarnovers to create a hole or eyelet, producing an increase and then decreasing to maintain the same stitch count. The way a yarnover is made varies depending on whether the stitch just worked and the next stitch are knit or purl stitches. In the US they are all called "yarnover" and are abbreviated to "yo," but in the UK the four different methods have separate names and abbreviations.

Just one yarnover method is used in this lace pattern (yarnover between purl and knit stitches), but all four are explained here so that you can easily understand how they work.

Yarnover between knit stitches

In the UK this method is called "yarn forward" and is abbreviated to "yfwd" or "yf." Be aware that "yf" can also be used to indicate that the yarn should be brought forward between the tips of the needles, as it sometimes is when slipping stitches.

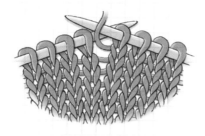

1 Work to the position of the yarnover. Bring the yarn to the front, between the tips of the needles.

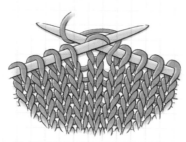

2 Take the yarn over the right-hand needle to the back and knit the next stitch on the left-hand needle. The loop of yarn made over the right-hand needle is the yarnover.

Yarnover between purl stitches

In the UK this version of a yarnover is called "yarn round needle" and is abbreviated to "yrn." The yarn is wrapped right around the right-hand needle, so you need to tension it firmly to prevent the yarnover being baggy once the next stitch has been purled.

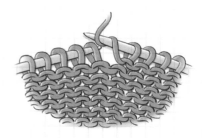

1 Work to the position of the yarnover. Wrap the yarn over and right around the right-hand needle.

2 Purl the next stitch on the left-hand needle. The loop of yarn made over the right-hand needle is the yarnover.

Yarnover between knit and purl stitches

In the UK this yarnover is called "yarn forward round needle" and is abbreviated to "yfrn." The yarn is wrapped right around the right-hand needle, so you need to tension it firmly to prevent the yarnover being baggy once the next stitch has been purled.

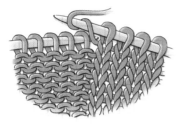

1 Work to the position of the yarnover. Bring the yarn to the front, between the tips of the needles, and wrap it over and right around the right-hand needle.

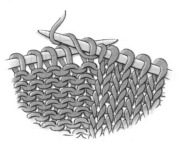

2 Purl the next stitch on the left-hand needle. The loop of yarn made over the right-hand needle is the yarnover.

Yarnover between purl and knit stitches

In the UK this version of a yarnover is called "yarn over needle" or "yarnover" and abbreviated to "yon" or "yo." However, be aware that if you are following a US pattern and the instruction is "yo," it only means this particular yarnover if there is a purl stitch before it and a knit stitch after it.

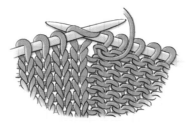

1 Work to the position of the yarnover. Leaving the yarn at the front of the work, insert the needle knitwise into the next stitch on the left-hand needle.

2 Take the yarn over the right-hand needle to the back and knit the stitch. The loop of yarn made over the right-hand needle is the yarnover.

ROMPERS

There is something so endearing about rompers, with their vintage nursery feel. This set has a garter stitch yoke with straps that adjust by moving the buttons when required, and a buttoned gusset for diaper changing. The ribs on the legs are picked up around the shaped edge after knitting the body.

Measurements
To fit ages

3–6	6–9	9–12	months

Finished measurements
(over diaper)

20	22	24½	in

Length
(from crotch to shoulder)

14¼	15¼	16½	in

Materials
3(3:3) x 1¾oz (50g) balls of Debbie Bliss Baby Cashmerino in Mist 57
Pair of size US 3 knitting needles
5 buttons

Gauge
25 sts and 50 rows to 4in square over garter st using size US 3 needles

Abbreviations
rem   remain(ing)
Also see page 19

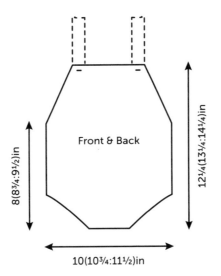

Front & Back

8(8¾:9½)in

12¼(13¼:14¼)in

10(10¾:11½)in

THE PATTERN

Back

With size US 3 needles, cast on 23(24:25) sts.
Beg with a p row, work in st st.
1st row (wrong side): P to end.
Cast on 4 sts at beg of next 8 rows and 6(8:10) sts at beg of foll 2 rows. *67(72:77) sts*
Work straight until piece measures 7½(8¼:9)in from
cast-on edge, ending with a wrong side row.
Dec row: K10(11:12), k2tog, [k13(14:15), k2tog] 3 times, k10(11:12). *63(68:73) sts*
Now work in garter st as follows:
K 3 rows.
Place a marker at each end of last row **.
Shape top
Dec row (right side): K7, skpo, k to last 9 sts, k2tog, k7.
K 3 rows.
Rep the last 4 rows 12(13:14) times and the dec row again. *35(38:41) sts*
K 2 rows.
Divide for straps
Next row (wrong side): K7, bind off 21(24:27) sts, k to end, leaving the first set of 7 sts on a holder or safety pin and cont on the second set of 7 sts.
K 50 rows on these 7 sts.
Bind off.
With right side facing, rejoin yarn to rem 7 sts on holder.
K 50 rows on these 7 sts.
Bind off.

Front

Work as given for Back to **.
Shape top
Dec row (right side): K7, skpo, k to last 9 sts, k2tog, k7.
K 3 rows.
Rep the last 4 rows 11(12:13) times and the dec row again. *37(40:43) sts*
K 1 row.
Buttonhole row: K2, k2tog, yf, k to last 4 sts, yf, skpo, k2.
K 1 row.
Dec row: K7, skpo, k to last 9 sts, k2tog, k7.
K 2 rows.
Bind off.

Leg borders

Join side seams to markers.
With right side facing and size US 3 needles, pick up and k52(56:62) sts evenly around edge of leg opening.
Picking up stitches evenly around a curved edge (page 77)
Rib row: [K1, p1] to end.
This row forms the rib and is repeated.
Rib a further 4 rows.
Bind off in rib.

Back crotch edging

With right side facing and size US 3 needles, pick up and k29(29:31) sts along row ends of leg borders and cast-on edges.
Picking up stitches evenly along a row edge (page 77)
Picking up stitches evenly along a cast-on or bound-off edge (page 77)
1st row: K1, [p1, k1] to end.
2nd row: P1, [k1, p1] to end.
3rd row: K1, [p1, k1] to end.
Bind off in rib.

Front crotch edging

With right side facing and size US 3 needles, pick up and k29(29:31) sts along row ends of leg borders and cast-on edges.
1st row: K1, [p1, k1] to end.
2nd buttonhole row: P1, k1, p1, yrn, p2tog, rib 8(8:9), work 2tog, yrn, rib 9(9:10), work 2tog, yrn, p1, k1, p1.
Pattern note: Working two together in rib (page 77)
3rd row: K1, [p1, k1] to end.
Bind off in rib.

To make up

Weave in all ends.
Sew on buttons.

THE TECHNIQUES

Picking up stitches evenly around a curved edge

This technique will usually be used when you are picking up stitches from a shaped edge to make a neckband or collar.

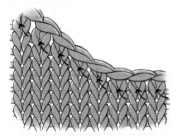

1 Insert the needle into the stitches one row below the bound-off edge, and not between the stitches because this may form a hole, unless you need more stitches than you have rows. Wrap the yarn around the needle and pull a loop through. Keep the line of picked-up stitches running in a smooth curve to make a neat top edge to the rib section.

Picking up stitches evenly along a row edge

You need to take into account the fact that a knitted stitch is wider than it is tall when picking up along the row edge of a piece of knitting.

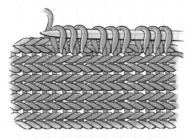

1 Put the needle into the space between the edge stitch and the next stitch. Wrap the yarn around the needle and pull a loop through. As the stitches you are picking up are wider than the rows you are picking them up from, after every third picked-up stitch, skip one row.

Picking up stitches evenly along a cast-on or bound-off edge

The principle is the same for either type of edge, though it is shown here on a bound-off edge.

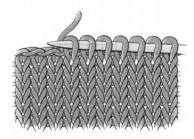

1 Put the needle into the stitch immediately below the bound-off edge and pull a loop through. In this way the new stitches will grow smoothly out of the old ones. When picking up along a cast-on edge, put the needle into the stitches of the cast-on row.

Pattern note: Working two together in rib

When decreasing in rib, work two together depending on what the next stitch will be. For example, if it is knit, knit two together, if purl, purl two together.

CLASSIC
CARDIGAN

This very classic cardigan is a wardrobe staple and uses techniques you have learned previously: stockinette stitch, rib, shaping, buttonholes, and picking up stitches on an edge. It has a square, set-in armhole where the top of the sleeve is slotted into the bound-off edges on the body.

Measurements

To fit ages

0–3	3–6	6–9	9–12	12–18	18–24	months

Finished measurements

19¼	20½	21¾	22¾	24	25½	in

Length to shoulder

9½	10¼	11	12	12½	13½	in

Sleeve length

5	6	6¾	7½	8¼	9½	in

Materials

3(3:4:4:4:5) x 1¾oz (50g) balls of Debbie Bliss Baby Cashmerino in Ecru 101

Pair each of size US 2 or 3 and size US 3 knitting needles

6(6:6:7:7:7) buttons

Gauge

25 sts and 34 rows to 4in square over st st using size US 3 needles

Abbreviations

See page 19

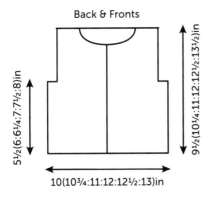

Back & Fronts

5½(6:6¼:7:7½:8)in

9½(10¼:11:12:12½:13½)in

10(10¾:11:12:12½:13)in

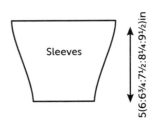

Sleeves

5(6:6¾:7½:8¼:9½)in

THE PATTERN

Back

With size US 2 or 3 needles, cast on 63(67:71:75:79:83) sts.

1st rib row: K1, [p1, k1] to end.
2nd rib row: P1, [k1, p1] to end.
These 2 rows form rib and are repeated 3 times more.
Change to size US 3 needles.
Beg with a k row, work in st st until back measures 5½(6:6¼:7:7½:8)in from cast-on edge, ending with a p row.

Shape armholes
Bind off 5(6:7:8:9:10) sts at beg of next 2 rows.
53(55:57:59:61:63) sts
Beg with a k row, work 36(38:40:42:46:50) rows in st st, ending with a p row.

Shape shoulders
Bind off 11(12:13:13:14:14) sts at beg of next 2 rows.
Leave rem 31(31:31:33:33:35) sts on a holder.
Pattern note: Putting stitches on a holder (see right)

Left front

With size US 2 or 3 needles, cast on 31(33:35:37:39:41) sts.

1st rib row: P1, [k1, p1] to end.
2nd rib row: K1, [p1, k1] to end.
Rep the last 2 rows 3 times more.
Change to size US 3 needles.
Beg with a k row, work in st st until front measures 5½(6:6¼:7:7½:8)in from cast-on edge, ending with a p row.

Shape armhole
Next row (right side): Bind off 5(6:7:8:9:10) sts, k to end.
26(27:28:29:30:31) sts

Beg with a p row, work 23(25:27:27:31:33) rows in st st, so ending with a p row.

Shape neck
Next row (right side): K to last 10(10:10:11:11:12) sts, leave these sts on a holder for neckband, turn and work on rem 16(17:18:18:19:19) sts for side of neck.
Next row: P to end.
Next row: K to last 2 sts, skpo.
Rep the last 2 rows 4 times.
11(12:13:13:14:14) sts
Work 3(3:3:3:5:7) rows.
Shape shoulder
Bind off.

Right front

With size US 2 or 3 needles, cast on 31(33:35:37:39:41) sts.

1st rib row: P1, [k1, p1] to end.
2nd rib row: K1, [p1, k1] to end.
Rep the last 2 rows 3 times more.
Change to size US 3 needles.
Beg with a k row, work in st st until front measures 5½(6:6¼:7:7½:8) in from cast-on edge, ending with a k row.

Shape armhole
Next row (wrong side): Bind off 5(6:7:8:9:10) sts, p to end.
26(27:28:29:30:31) sts
Beg with a k row, work 22(24:26:26:30:32) rows in st st, so ending with a p row.
Shape neck
Next row (right side):
K10(10:10:11:11:12) sts, leave these sts on a holder, k to end.
Cont on rem 16(17:18:18:19:19) sts for side of neck.
Next row: P to end.

Pattern note: Putting stitches on a holder

Stitches are placed on a stitch holder so that they can be left "live" and worked later on. If you only have a few stitches that need to be separated out from the rest of the work, you can use a safety pin. If you need to hold a lot of stitches and don't want to bunch them up on a holder, you can thread the stitches through a strand of yarn. This also means that if you are not using a double-pointed stitch holder you can slip the stitches back onto the needle from either end of the strand.

Slip the stitches from your needle purlwise (put the point of the holder from right to left into the stitch) onto the holder. This prevents the stitches from being twisted.

Next row: K2tog, k to end.
Rep the last 2 rows 4 times.
11(12:13:13:14:14) sts
Work 4(4:4:4:6:8) rows.
Shape shoulder
Bind off.

Sleeves

(Make 2)
With size US 2 or 3 needles, cast on
38(40:44:46:50:54) sts.
Rib row: [K1, p1] to end.
This row forms the rib and is
repeated 7 times more.
Change to size US 3 needles.
Beg with a k row, work in st st
as folls:
Work 4 rows.
Inc row: K3, m1, k to last 3 sts,
m1, k3.
Work 3 rows.
Rep the last 4 rows 6(7:8:10:11:12)
times more and the inc row again.
54(58:64:70:76:82) sts
Cont straight until sleeve
measures 5(6:6¾:7½:8¼:9½)in
from cast-on edge, ending with
a p row.
Place a marker at each end of
last row.
Work a further 8(8:10:10:12:12) rows.
Bind off.

Neckband

Join shoulder seams.
With right side facing and size US 2
or 3 needles, slip 10(10:10:11:11:12)
sts from right front neck holder
onto a needle, pick up and
k17(17:17:19:19:19) sts up right
front neck, k31(31:31:33:33:35) sts

from back neck holder, pick up
and k17(17:17:19:19:19) sts down
left front neck, k10(10:10:11:11:12)
sts from left front holder.
85(85:85:93:93:97) sts
*Pattern note: Slipping stitches from
a holder onto a needle (see right)*
1st rib row: K1, [p1, k1] to end.
2nd rib row: P1, [k1, p1] to end.
3rd row: As 1st rib row.
Bind off in rib.

Button band

With right side facing and size
US 2 or 3 needles, pick up and
k55(59:65:69:75:81) sts along
left front edge.
Work 3 rows in rib as given
for neckband.
Bind off in rib.

Buttonhole band

With right side facing and size
US 2 or 3 needles, pick up and
k55(59:65:69:75:81) sts along right
front edge.
Work 1 row in rib as given for
neckband.
Buttonhole row: Rib 4(3:4:3:3:3),
[rib 2 tog, yf, rib 7(8:9:10:9:10) sts]
5(5:5:5:6:6) times, rib 2 tog, yf, rib 4.
Rib 1 row.
Bind off in rib.

Pattern note: Slipping stitches from a holder onto a needle

To return the stitches on your
holder or waste yarn onto your
needle, slip them knitwise (put the
point of the needle from left to
right into the stitch).

Rather than transferring the stitches
from your holder back onto a
needle, you can work them straight
from the holder in the same way as
you would from a needle.

To make up

With center of bound-off edge
of sleeve to shoulder seam, sew
sleeves into armholes, easing to fit
and with row ends above sleeve
markers sewn to sts bound off at
underarm.
*Mattress stitch on stockinette stitch:
joining stitches to row ends (see
opposite)*
Join side and sleeve seams.
Weave in all ends.
Sew on buttons.

THE TECHNIQUES

Mattress stitch on stockinette stitch: joining stitches to row ends

This is a combination of the techniques for sewing stitches to stitches (page 67) and row ends to row ends (page 56). The spacing of the sewn stitches on the row-end edge might take some experimentation, but the aim is to get the sewn stitches all lying flat without puckering. This seam is used when sewing the top of sleeves to the body in a dropped shoulder or square set-in sleeve.

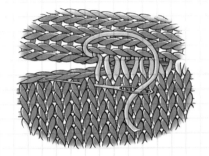

2 On the cast-on or bound-off edge, take the needle under two stitch loops.

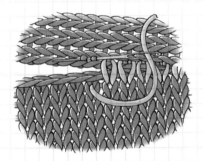

3 However, as a stitch is wider than it is long, on approximately every third stitch along the row-end edge, take the needle under two bars instead of one.

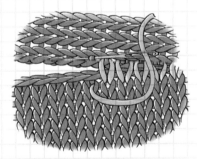

1 Right sides up, lay the two edges to be joined touching one another. Pin them together at the halfway point to help space the sewn stitches neatly. Thread a blunt-tipped sewing needle with a long length of yarn. Secure the yarn on the back of either piece. On the row-end edge, take the needle under one bar of yarn either a whole stitch in from the edge, or half a stitch, as shown here.

PATCHWORK
BLANKET

All knitted stitch patterns are made from knit or purl stitches, and there are some simple ones that combine the two to produce lovely fabrics. The blanket here is made using my favorite patterns in a patchwork design. Making it is the perfect way to practice creating texture without having to concentrate on shaping as you would in a garment.

Measurements
Approximately 25½ x 28¾in

Materials
8 x 1¾oz (50g) balls of Debbie Bliss Cashmerino Aran in Stone 27
Pair of size US 7 knitting needles or size US 7 circular needle 32in long

Gauge
21 sts and 32 rows to 4in square over seed stitch using size US 7 needles

Abbreviations
See page 19

Notes
Each pattern square is worked over 29 sts and 38 rows. As the blanket pattern involves working rows from different blocks in turn, you may find it helps to photocopy the block patterns and lay them out in sequence as needed. That way you can read off the rows without having to turn pages in the book. And if you are new to texture knitting and are worried about making mistakes, you can add lifelines to your squares.
Putting in a lifeline (page 90)
Unraveling to a lifeline (page 90)
You may find it easier to use a circular needle rather than straight needles as you will be working on 135 sts throughout, but you need to work backward and forward on the circular needle, not in rounds.
Pattern note: Working in rows on a circular needle (page 91)
When starting a new ball of yarn, do not join in on the edge; instead, join between the seed st edge and the first or last texture square.
Pattern note: Joining in a yarn (page 91)

THE PATTERN

Pattern square A—tumbling blocks

1st row (right side): K to end.
2nd row: K1, [p1, k1] to end.
3rd row: * P2, [k1, p1] 3 times, k2; rep from * once more, p2, [k1, p1] 3 times, k1.
4th row: * P2, [k1, p1] twice, k3, p1; rep from * once more, p2, [k1, p1] twice, k3.
5th row: [P4, k1, p1, k4] twice, p4, k1, p1, k3.
6th row: P4, [k5, p5] twice, k5.
7th row: [P5, k5] twice, p5, k4.
8th row: [P4, k4, p1, k1] twice, p4, k4, p1.
9th row: [P1, k1, p3, k3, p1, k1] twice, p1, k1, p3, k3, p1.
10th row: * P1, k1, p2, k2, [p1, k1] twice; rep from * once more, p1, k1, p2, k2, p1, k1, p1.
11th row: P1, [k1, p1] to end.
12th row: As 11th row.
13th row: [P1, k1, p1, k2, p2, k1, p1, k1] twice, p1, k1, p1, k2, p2, k1, p1.
14th row: [P1, k3, p3, k1, p1, k1] twice, p1, k1, p3, k3, p1, k1.
15th row: [P1, k4, p4, k1] twice, p1, k4, p4.
16th row: K4, [p5, k5] twice, p5.
17th row: [K5, p5] twice, k5, p4.
18th row: K3, p1, k1, p4, [k4, p1, k1, p4] twice.
19th row: * K3, [p1, k1] twice, p3; rep from * once more, k3, [p1, k1] twice, p2.
20th row: K1, [p1, k1] 3 times, p2, * k2, [p1, k1] 3 times, p2; rep from * once more.
21st row: K1, [p1, k1] to end.
22nd to 37th rows: Rep 2nd to 17th rows once more.
38th row: P to end.
These 38 rows form patt A.

Pattern square B—garter stitch vertical zigzags

1st row (right side): K to end.
2nd and every foll wrong side row: P to end.
3rd row: K6, [p3, k3] 3 times, p3, k2.
5th row: K5, [p3, k3] 4 times.
7th row: K4, [p3, k3] 4 times, k1.
9th row: K3, [p3, k3] 4 times, k2.
11th row: K2, [p3, k3] 4 times, k3.
13th row: As 9th row.
15th row: As 7th row.
17th row: As 5th row.
18th row: P to end.
19th to 34th rows: Rep 3rd to 18th rows once more.
35th row: As 3rd row.
36th row: P to end.
37th to 38th rows: As 1st and 2nd rows.
These 38 rows form patt B.

Pattern square C—double lattice

1st row (right side): K to end.
2nd row: P1, [k1, p1, k1, p9] twice, [k1, p1] twice.
3rd row: K2, p1, k1, p1, k7, [p1, k1] twice, p1, k7, p1, k1, p1, k2.
4th row: P3, k1, p1, k1, p5, k1, [p1, k1] 3 times, p5, k1, p1, k1, p3.
5th row: K4, [p1, k1, p1, k3] 4 times, k1.
6th row: * P5, k1, [p1, k1] 3 times; rep from * once more, p5.
7th row: K6, p1, [k1, p1] twice, k7, p1, [k1, p1] twice, k6.
8th row: P7, k1, p1, k1, p9, k1, p1, k1, p7.
9th row: As 7th row.
10th row: As 6th row.
11th row: As 5th row.
12th row: As 4th row.
13th row: As 3rd row.
14th to 37th rows: Rep 2nd to 13th rows twice more.
38th row: P to end.
These 38 rows form patt C.

Pattern square D—seed stitch horizontal zigzags

1st row (right side): K to end.
2nd row: P2, [k1, p7] 3 times, k1, p2.
3rd row: [K1, p1] twice, [k5, p1, k1, p1] 3 times, k1.
4th row: * K1, [p1, k1] twice, p3; rep from * twice more, k1, [p1, k1] twice.
5th row: K1, [p1, k1] to end.
6th row: K1, *p3, k1, [p1, k1] twice; rep from * twice more, p3, k1.
7th row: K5, [p1, k1, p1, k5] 3 times.
8th row: P6, [k1, p7] twice, k1, p6.
9th row: K2, [p1, k7] 3 times, p1, k2.
10th row: [P1, k1] twice, [p5, k1, p1, k1] 3 times, p1.
11th row: * P1, [k1, p1] twice, k3; rep from * twice more, p1, [k1, p1] twice.
12th row: P1, [k1, p1] to end.
13th row: P1, * k3, p1, [k1, p1] twice; rep from * twice more, k3, p1.
14th row: P5, [k1, p1, k1, p5] 3 times.
15th row: K6, [p1, k7] twice, p1, k6.
16th to 29th rows: Rep 2nd to 15th rows once more.
30th to 36th rows: Rep 2nd to 8th rows once more.
37th row: K to end.
38th row: P to end.
These 38 rows form patt D.

Pattern square E—seed stitch woven squares

1st row (right side): K to end.
2nd row: P to end.
3rd row: [K1, p1] 3 times, * k2, p1, [k1, p1] twice; rep from * twice more, k2.
4th row: P3, [k1, p1, k1, p4] 3 times, k1, p1, k1, p2.
5th to 8th rows: Rep 3rd and 4th rows twice more.
9th row: K1, [p12, k2] twice.
10th row: [P2, k12] twice, p1.
11th row: K to end.
12th row: * P2, k1, [p1, k1] twice; rep from * 3 times more, p1.
13th row: K2, [p1, k1, p1, k4] 3 times, p1, k1, p1, k3.
14th to 17th rows: Rep 12th and 13th rows twice more.
18th row: K7, p2, k12, p2, k6.
19th row: P6, k2, p12, k2, p7.
20th row: P to end.
21st to 38th rows: Rep 3rd to 20th rows once more.
These 38 rows form patt E.

Blanket

With size US 7 needles or circular needle, cast on 135 sts.

Seed st row: K1, [p1, k1] to end.

This row forms seed st and is repeated 5 times more.

Seed stitch (page 91)

1st line of pattern squares

1st row (right side): K1, [p1, k1] twice, work across 1st row of A, k1, p1, k1, work across 1st row of B, k1, p1, k1, work across 1st row of C, k1, p1, k1, work across 1st row of D, k1, [p1, k1] twice.

2nd row: K1, [p1, k1] twice, work across 2nd row of D, k1, p1, k1, work across 2nd row of C, k1, p1, k1, work across 2nd row of B, k1, p1, k1, work across 2nd row of A, k1, [p1, k1] twice.

These 2 rows set the positions of 4 of the 5 pattern squares with seed st at each end and between the squares.

3rd to 38th rows: Working correct rows of squares, rep 1st and 2nd rows.

Work 6 rows in seed st.

2nd line of pattern squares

1st row (right side): K1, [p1, k1] twice, work across 1st row of C, k1, p1, k1, work across 1st row of A, k1, p1, k1, work across 1st row of D, k1, p1, k1, work across 1st row of E, k1, [p1, k1] twice.

2nd row: K1, [p1, k1] twice, work across 2nd row of E, k1, p1, k1, work across 2nd row of D, k1, p1, k1, work across 2nd row of A, k1, p1, k1, work across 2nd row of C,

k1, [p1, k1] twice.

These 2 rows set the positions of 4 of the 5 pattern squares with seed st at each end and between the squares.

3rd to 38th rows: Working correct rows of squares, rep 1st and 2nd rows.

Work 6 rows in seed st.

3rd line of pattern squares

1st row (right side): K1, [p1, k1] twice, work across 1st row of D, k1, p1, k1, work across 1st row of E, k1, p1, k1, work across 1st row of C, k1, p1, k1, work across 1st row of B, k1, [p1, k1] twice.

2nd row: K1, [p1, k1] twice, work across 2nd row of B, k1, p1, k1, work across 2nd row of C, k1, p1, k1, work across 2nd row of E, k1, p1, k1, work across 2nd row of D, k1, [p1, k1] twice.

These 2 rows set the positions of 4 of the 5 pattern squares with seed st at each end and between the squares.

3rd to 38th rows: Working correct rows of squares, rep 1st and 2nd rows.

Work 6 rows in seed st.

4th line of pattern squares

1st row (right side): K1, [p1, k1] twice, work across 1st row of B, k1, p1, k1, work across 1st row of A, k1, p1, k1, work across 1st row of D, k1, p1, k1, work across 1st row of E, k1, [p1, k1] twice.

2nd row: K1, [p1, k1] twice, work across 2nd row of E, k1, p1, k1, work across 2nd row of D, k1, p1, k1, work across 2nd row of A, k1,

p1, k1, work across 2nd row of B, k1, [p1, k1] twice.

These 2 rows set the positions of 4 of the 5 pattern squares with seed st at each end and between the squares.

3rd to 38th rows: Working correct rows of squares, rep 1st and 2nd rows.

Work 6 rows in seed st.

5th line of pattern squares

1st row (right side): K1, [p1, k1] twice, work across 1st row of E, k1, p1, k1, work across 1st row of B, k1, p1, k1, work across 1st row of C, k1, p1, k1, work across 1st row of A, k1, [p1, k1] twice.

2nd row: K1, [p1, k1] twice, work across 2nd row of A, k1, p1, k1, work across 2nd row of C, k1, p1, k1, work across 2nd row of B, k1, p1, k1, work across 2nd row of E, k1, [p1, k1] twice.

These 2 rows set the positions of 4 of the 5 pattern squares with seed st at each end and between the squares.

3rd to 38th rows: Working correct rows of squares, rep 1st and 2nd rows.

Work 5 rows in seed st.

Bind off in seed stitch.

To make up

Weave in all ends.

Block or lightly press the blanket, being careful not to over-flatten the seed stitch sections.

THE TECHNIQUES

Putting in a lifeline

There are two reasons for putting in a lifeline: either you've made a mistake and need to unravel, or the pattern is complicated and you think you might make a mistake.

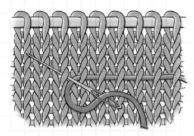

1 If you realize you have made a mistake in your knitting and you need to unravel several rows, you can put in a lifeline before you pull the rows out to help you pick up the stitches again easily. Thread a blunt-tipped sewing needle with a length of waste yarn that's longer than the knitting is wide. Pass the needle through the right-hand leg of each stitch in the row you need to unravel to, being careful not to split the yarn with the needle.

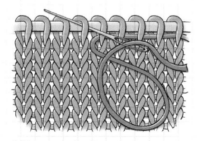

2 If you are about to start on a more complicated part of a pattern, then you can put in a lifeline on the current row, just in case. Thread a blunt-tipped sewing needle with a length of waste yarn that's longer than the knitting is wide, and just slide it through the stitches on the needle. Regular lifelines can be a good idea on complicated lace patterns, which are very difficult to accurately pick up stitches in if you have to unravel.

Unraveling to a lifeline

It is very simple (although always somewhat frustrating) to unravel knitting if a lifeline is in place.

1 Take the knitting off the needle and pull out the yarn to unravel the rows. The lifeline will prevent rows unraveling beyond it, and will hold all the stitches facing in the right direction.

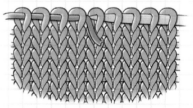

2 Following the path of the lifeline, slip each stitch in turn onto a knitting needle, pulling out the waste yarn as you go. Be sure to put the stitches back on the needle in the right direction, so that the working yarn is at the tip of the needle, ready to work the next row.

Seed stitch

This is an ideal fabric for edgings and collars as it lies flat and has a lovely texture that adds simple detail to any project. As with single rib, seed stitch is worked by alternately knitting and purling stitches across a row, but on subsequent rows the stitches that were purled on the previous row are purled again, and vice versa.

The exact pattern depends on whether the seed stitch is being worked over an even or odd number of stitches.

For an even number of stitches
1st row: [K1, p1] to end.
2nd row: [P1, k1] to end.
Rep 1st and 2nd rows as required.

For an odd number of stitches
1st row: [K1, p1] to last st, k1.
Rep 1st row as required.

Pattern note: Working in rows on a circular needle

If you are going to be working on a large number of stitches, it is sometimes easier to use a circular needle rather than trying to force all the stitches onto straight needles. You use the circular needle in exactly the same way as straight needles as follows: when working a right-side row, hold one point of the needle in your right hand and the other point in your left hand, work the stitches from the left-hand needle onto the right-hand needle exactly as you would on straight needles, then once you have worked all the stitches, simply turn the work and hold what was the right-hand point in your left hand and the left-hand point in your right hand, and work the next row.

If you are working on straight needles and need to leave your work for a few hours, overnight, or for days at a time, slip all the stitches onto a circular needle: you are far less likely to get an obvious line across your work if you do this rather than leaving them on a straight needle.

Pattern note: Joining in a new yarn

It is sometimes neater to join in a new ball of yarn a few stitches in from the edge, particularly if the edge will not form part of a seam. In this project, at the start of a new row, work the seed stitch edge stitches, then start a new ball, or work across the row to the end of the patterning and join in the new ball before working the seed stitch edge. This means that you will have a lovely clean edge on the blanket and the yarn ends will be tucked away and hidden.

COAT

Knitted in my favorite seed stitch, this double-breasted coat has a Peter Pan collar, inset pockets, and a half belt. Turning rows on the collar are used to create ease around the back of the neck and to stop the collar pulling back. The pocket linings are knitted in a contrast color to give a pop along the opening—very smart!

Measurements

To fit ages

0–3	3–6	6–9	9–12	12–18	18–24	months

Finished measurements

Chest

19	20½	22½	24	26	28	in

Length to shoulder

10	11	12¼	13½	15	16½	in

Sleeve length
(with cuff turned back)

5	6	6¾	7½	8¼	9	in

Materials

5(5:5:6:6:7) x 1¾oz (50g) balls of Debbie Bliss Rialto DK in Indigo 51 (M)
1 x 1¾oz (50g) ball of Debbie Bliss Baby Cashmerino in Wasabi 313 (C)
Pair each of size US 3 and size US 6 knitting needles
8 buttons

Gauge

22 sts and 35 rows to 4in square over seed st using size US 6 needles

Abbreviations

DK double knit
Also see page 19

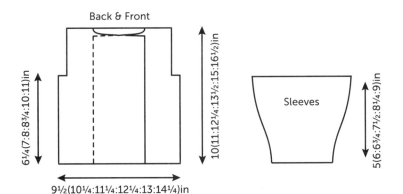

Back & Front

6¼(7:8:8¾:10:11)in

10(11:12¼:13½:15:16½)in

9½(10¼:11¼:12¼:13:14¼)in

Sleeves

5(6:6¾:7½:8¼:9)in

THE PATTERN

Back

With size US 6 needles and M, cast on 53(57:63:67:73:79) sts.
Seed st row: K1, [p1, k1] to end.
This row forms the seed st and is repeated.
Cont in seed st until back measures 6¼(7:8:8¾:10:11)in from cast-on edge, ending with a wrong side row.
Shape armholes
Bind off 4(4:4:4:5:6) sts at beg of next 2 rows.
45(49:55:59:63:67) sts
Cont straight until back measures 10(11:12¼:13½:15:16½)in from cast-on edge, ending with a wrong side row.
Shape shoulders
Bind off 11(12:14:15:16:17) sts at beg of next 2 rows.
Bind off rem 23(25:27:29:31:33) sts.

Pocket linings

(Make 2)
With size US 3 needles and C, cast on 14(15:16:17:18:19) sts.
Beg with a k row, work 22(24:26:28:30:32) rows in st st, ending with a p row.
Next row: K3, k2tog, k4(5:6:7:8:9), k2tog, k3. 12(13:14:15:16:17) sts.
Leave these sts on a holder.

Left front

With size US 6 needles and M, cast on 38(41:45:48:52:56) sts.
1st seed st row: [K1, p1] to last 0(1:1:0:0:0) sts, k0(1:1:0:0:0).
2nd seed st row: K0(1:1:0:0:0), [p1, k1] to end.
These 2 rows form the seed st and are repeated 15(16:18:20:23:26) times more, ending with a wrong side row.
Place pocket
Horizontal inset pocket (page 98)
Next row (right side): Seed st 3, bind off next 12(13:14:15:16:17) sts, seed st to end.
Next row: Seed st 23(25:28:30:33:36), p across 12(13:14:15:16:17) sts of pocket lining, seed st 3.
Cont in seed st across all sts until front measures 6¼(7:8:8¾:10:11) in from cast-on edge, ending with a wrong side row.
Shape armhole
Bind off 4(4:4:4:5:6) sts at beg of next row. *34(37:41:44:47:50) sts*
Cont straight until front measures 8¼(9½:10¾:12:13½:15)in from cast-on edge, ending with a right side row.
Shape neck
Next row (wrong side): Bind off 18(20:22:24:26:28) sts, patt to end. *16(17:19:20:21:22) sts*
Dec 1 st at neck edge on next 5 rows. *11(12:14:15:16:17) sts*
Work straight until front measures the same as back to shoulder, ending at armhole edge.

Shape shoulder

Next row: Bind off.
Marking button positions
On the Left Front, mark the position for 3 pairs of buttons, the first pair ¾in down from neck edge, the second pair 2(2¼:2¾:3¼:3½:4)in below the first pair and the third pair 2(2¼:2¾:3¼:3½:4)in below the second pair.
When working the Right Front, work buttonholes to match markers as follows:
Buttonhole row: Seed st 3, yrn, p2tog, seed st 13(15:17:19:21:23), p2tog, yrn, seed st to end.

Right front

With size US 6 needles and M, cast on 38(41:45:48:52:56) sts.
1st seed st row: K0(1:1:0:0:0), [p1, k1] to end.
2nd seed st row: [K1, p1] to last 0(1:1:1:1:1) sts, k0(1:1:1:1:1).
These 2 rows form seed st and are repeated 15(16:18:20:23:26) times more, ending with a wrong side row.
Seed st a further 30(32:36:40:46:52) rows, ending with a wrong side row.
Place pocket
Next row (right side): Seed st 23(25:28:30:33:36), bind off next 12(13:14:15:16:17) sts, seed st 3.

Next row: Seed st 3, p across 12(13:14:15:16:17) sts of pocket lining, seed st to end.

Cont in seed st across all sts until front measures 6¼(7:8:8¾:10:11)in from cast-on edge, ending with a right side row.

Shape armhole

Bind off 4(4:4:4:5:6) sts at beg of next row. *34(37:41:44:47:50) sts*

Cont straight until front measures 8¼(9½:10¾:12:13½:15)in from cast-on edge, ending with a wrong side row.

Shape neck

Next row: Bind off 18(20:22:24:26:28) sts, patt to end. *16(17:19:20:21:22) sts*

Dec 1 st at neck edge on next 5 rows. *11(12:14:15:16:17) sts*

Work straight until front measures the same as back to shoulder, ending at armhole edge.

Shape shoulder

Next row: Bind off.

Sleeves

(Make 2)

With size US 6 needles and M, cast on 29(31:35:37:41:45) sts.

Seed st row: K1, [p1, k1] to end.

This row forms the seed st and is repeated 9(11:11:13:13:15) times more.

Change to size US 3 needles.

Place a marker at each end of last row.

Seed st 8(10:10:12:12:14) rows.

Change to size US 6 needles.

Inc and work into seed st, 1 st at each end of the next row and every foll 6th row, until there are 41(45:51:55:61:67) sts.

Pattern note: Increasing in seed stitch (page 98)

Cont straight until sleeve measures 5(6:6¾:7½:8¼:9)in from markers,

ending with a wrong side row.

Place a marker at each end of last row.

Work a further 6 rows.

Bind off.

Collar

Join shoulder seams.

With right side facing, size US 3 needles and M, miss first 13(14:15:16:17:18) sts bind off at right front neck, pick up and k 1 st into each of rem 5(6:7:8:9:10) bound-off sts, then 10 sts along row ends to shoulder, cast on 33(33:35:37:37) sts, pick up and k10 sts along row ends of left front neck from shoulder to bound-off edge, k1 st into each of first 5(6:7:8:9:10) bound off sts. *63(65:69:71:75:77) sts*

Seed st row: K1, [p1, k1] to end.

This row forms the seed st.

Next 2 rows: Seed st to last 18 sts, turn, seed st to last 18 sts, turn.

Pattern note: Turning rows (page 99)

Next 2 rows: Seed st to last 12 sts, turn, seed st to last 12 sts, turn.

Next 2 rows: Seed st to last 6 sts, turn, seed st to last 6 sts, turn.

Next row: Seed st to end.

Work 3 rows in seed st across all sts.

Change to size US 6 needles.

Seed st a further 11(11:13:13:1515) rows across all sts.

Bind off in seed st.

Belt

With size US 6 needles and M, cast on 35(39:43:45:49:53) sts.

Seed st row: K1, [p1, k1] to end.

This row forms the seed st.

Seed st a further 9(9:10:10:11:11) rows.

Bind off in seed st.

To make up

Easing in fullness, join cast-on edge of collar to sts bound off at back neck.

Pattern note: Easing in (page 99)

With center of bound-off edge of sleeve to shoulder, sew on sleeves, with row ends above markers sewn to sts cast bound off at underarm.

Join side and sleeve seams.

Flat seam (page 99)

Sew down pocket linings.

Weave in all ends.

Sew on buttons.

Secure belt to back by sewing on buttons through both thicknesses.

Pattern note: Increasing in seed stitch

Where there is shaping, when you are working in a stitch pattern you need to keep the pattern consistent. For example, when increasing on the sleeves here, work those increased stitches as knit or a purl depending on which stitch comes next in the pattern. On a more complicated stitch pattern it can be helpful to chart the stitches on some graph paper to keep track of which stitch comes next.

Horizontal inset pocket

The inset pocket, sometimes called an integrated pocket, is an easy and neat style. A contrast lining can add a flash of color that creates design detail, particularly if you don't add a border at the top edge of the pocket.

First, make a pocket lining. This should be a piece of knitting two stitches wider than the required width of the pocket opening, and one row deeper than the required depth, and should finish with a right-side row. Leave the stitches on a spare needle or a stitch holder.

1 Work to the row before the position of the top of the pocket, which should be a wrong-side row. On the next row, knit to the position of the pocket. Bind off the required number of stitches for the pocket opening, then knit to the end of the row.

2 On the next row, purl to one stitch before the bound-off stitches. Hold the lining with the wrong side facing you and purl the last stitch before the bind off together as one with the first stitch of the lining.

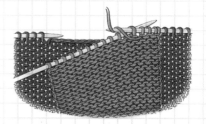

3 Purl across the lining stitches to the last stitch. Purl this stitch together with the first stitch on the left-hand needle after the bind off. Purl to the end of the row and complete the rest of the piece.

Slip stitch the pocket lining to the back of the piece.

Flat seam

This seam is particularly good for babies as there is no bulky seam to rub against skin. However, it is not a very strong seam and the stitches can stretch. It is worked on the wrong side.

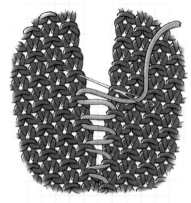

1 Wrong sides up, lay the two edges to be joined side by side. Thread a blunt-tipped sewing needle with a long length of yarn and secure the yarn on the back of one piece. Take the needle through the bump of the first edge stitch on one side, then through the same bump on the side of the other piece. Continue in this way, zigzagging between the stitch bumps, as shown, and pulling the seam gently tight as you work.

Pattern note: Turning rows

Turning rows can cause confusion even to a quite experienced knitter, but the technique is really simple. It literally means turning the work before the row is completed; this is why they are also referred to as short rows. The result is that part of the work has more rows than others, creating shaping that helps ease pieces such as collars around the neck.

Pattern note: Easing in

Some pieces, such as a hood or collar, need extra stitches to create fullness to prevent them being tight and uncomfortable around the back of the neck. This means that you will need to accommodate those extra stitches when you are sewing the collar or hood to the bound-off stitches of the back neck. This is done by slightly gathering the collar or hood to fit the neck edge as you sew the pieces together.

BOOTEES

Bootees always look the simplest items to make, but actually they are a little more complex as they involve turning rows to create the instep and sole. If you follow the instructions carefully, all will be clear. Knitted in garter stitch, the cuff turns over at the top and I have sewn blanket stitch on the cuff of these bootees for decoration.

Measurements
One size to fit 3–6 months

Materials
1 x 1¾oz (50g) of Debbie Bliss Baby Cashmerino in Denim, Mink, Wasabi or Light PInk
Pair of size US 2 or 3 knitting needles (see my note on page 49)

Gauge
26 sts and 56 rows to 4in square over garter stitch using size US 2 or 3 needles

Abbreviations
See page 19

THE PATTERN

Bootee

(Make 2)
With size US 2 or 3 needles, cast on 36 sts.
K 21 rows.
Shape instep
Next row: K24, turn.
Next row: K12, turn.
Cont on center 12 sts only, leave the 2 groups of 12 sts at each side on the needle.
Pattern note: Working on center group of stitches only (see left)
K 24 rows.
Break off yarn.
With right side facing and first group of 12 held sts on right-hand needle, rejoin yarn at base of instep, pick up and k12 sts along side edge of instep, k across 12 sts of instep, pick up and k12 sts along other side of instep, k rem 12 sts. *60 sts*
K 13 rows.
Break off yarn.
Shape sole
With right side facing, slip first 24 sts onto right-hand needle, rejoin yarn and k12, turn.
Next row: K11, k2tog, turn.
Rep last row until 24 sts rem, k to end.
Bind off.

To make up

Join back seam.
Weave in all ends.
Work a row of blanket stitch around the edge of the cuff, being careful not to pull it too tight and so affect the elasticity of the edge.
Blanket stitch (see right)

THE TECHNIQUES

Blanket stitch

This stitch may be used along an edge, or on the surface of knitted fabric. Work in either direction; shown here worked right to left.

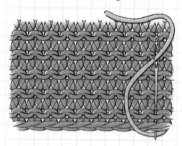

1 * Insert the needle from front to back and bring it back through to the front directly below where it went in, or below the edge of the knitting if you are embroidering along the edge.

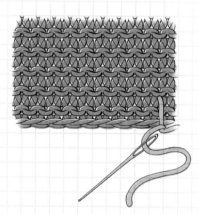

2 Pull the thread through, making sure that the working loop goes under the needle.

Pattern note: Working on center group of stitches only

In order to shape the top of the bootees, you will need to work on the 12 center stitches while keeping the first and last 12 stitches on the same needle. Simply turn the work as you would normally at the end of a row, and carry on working on the center 12 stitches to complete the 25 rows.

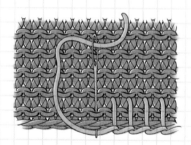

3 Repeat from *, spacing the blanket stitches evenly.

HOODED
SWEATER

The addition of a hood to a knit can make it look modern and sporty. It also has the advantage of adding extra warmth, and it doesn't go missing like a hat. The hood on this sweater is created by extending a shawl collar, folding it in half, and seaming the top. Easing in the fullness at the back neck makes a roomy, comfortable hood.

Measurements

To fit ages

6–12	12–18	18–24	months

Finished measurements

Chest

22	24¾	27½	in

Length to shoulder

11	12½	14½	in

Sleeve length
(with cuff turned back)

6¾	8	8¾	in

Materials

6(7:8) x 1¾oz (50g) balls of Debbie Bliss Rialto DK in Bark 87
Pair each of size US 5 and size US 6 needles
Size US 5 circular needle

Gauge

24 sts and 36 rows to 4in square over patt using size US 6 needles

Abbreviations

See page 19

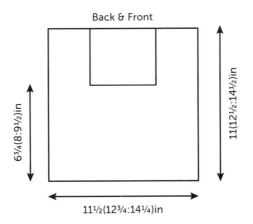

Back & Front

6¾(8:9½)in

11(12½:14½)in

11½(12¾:14¼)in

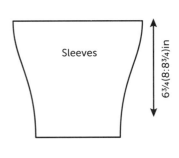

Sleeves

6¾(8:8¾)in

THE PATTERN

Back

With size US 5 needles, cast on 70(78:86) sts.

1st rib row (right side): K4, [p2, k2] to last 6 sts, p2, k4.

2nd rib row: K2, [p2, k2] to end.

These 2 rows form the double rib patt and are repeated.

Double rib (page 109)

Rep the last 2 rows for 2in, ending with a 2nd row.

Change to size US 6 needles and work in patt as follows:

1st row (right side): K2, [p2, k2] to end.

2nd row: P2, [k2, p2] to end.

3rd row: P2, [k2, p2] to end.

4th row: K2, [p2, k2] to end.

These 4 rows form the double seed st patt and are repeated.

Pattern note: Double seed stitch (see right)

Cont in patt until back measures 11(12½:14½)in from cast-on edge, ending with a wrong side row.

Shape shoulders

Bind off 19(21:23) sts at beg of next 2 rows.

Bind off rem 32(36:40) sts.

Front

Work as given for back until front measures 6¾(8:9½)in from cast-on edge, ending with a right side row.

Shape neck

Next row (wrong side): Patt 27(29:31) sts, bind off center 16(20:24) sts, patt to end.

Cont in patt on last set of 27(29:31) sts only for first side of neck until front measures the same as back to shoulder shaping, ending at side edge.

Next row: Bind off 19(21:23) sts, patt to end.

Next row: Patt 8 sts, and leave these 8 sts on a holder.

With right side facing, rejoin yarn to rem sts, patt to end.

Work in patt on these 27(29:31) sts for second side of neck until front measures the same as back to shoulder shaping, ending at side edge.

Next row: Bind off 19(21:23) sts, patt to end.

Next row: Patt 8 sts, and leave these 8 sts on a holder.

Sleeves

With size US 6 needles, cast on 42(46:50) sts.

1st rib row: P2, [k2, p2] to end.

2nd rib row: K2, [p2, k2] to end.

Rep the last 2 rows 7 times more.

Change to size US 5 needles.

Work a further 16 rows.

Change to size US 6 needles and work in patt as follows:

1st row: K2, [p2, k2] to end.

2nd row: P2, [k2, p2] to end.

3rd row: P2, [k2, p2] to end.

4th row: K2, [p2, k2] to end.

These 4 rows form the seed st patt and are repeated.

Pattern note: Double seed stitch

This very simple pattern gives good textural detail to the knitted fabric and works well with the double rib pattern.

THE TECHNIQUES

Double rib

This is a popular, chunky variation of single rib and is worked over an even number of stitches divisible by four, or four plus two stitches. It can be used in the same way as single rib, though it is less stretchy.

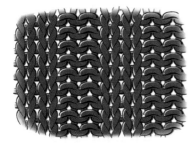

Number of stitches divisible by four
1st row : [K2, p2] to end.
Rep 1st row as required.

Number of stitches divisible by four plus two stitches
1st row: [K2, p2] to last 2 sts, k2.
2nd row: [P2, k2] to last 2 sts, p2.
Rep 1st and 2nd rows as required.

Inc and work into patt 1 st at each end of the next row and 7(9:11) foll 4th rows. *58(66:74) sts*
Cont straight until sleeve measures 8¼(9½:10¾)in from cast-on edge, ending with a wrong side row.
Bind off.

Hood

With right side facing and size US 6 needles, slip 8 sts on right front neck holder onto a needle, cast on 52(56:60) sts, then with right side of front facing, starting at shoulder edge, patt across 8 sts on left front neck holder. *68(72:76) sts*
Work in patt, as set for 7½(8:8¼)in, ending with a wrong side row.
Shape top
Next row: Patt 34(36:38) sts, turn and work on these sts only for first side of hood.
Bind off 5 sts at beg of next row and 4 foll wrong side rows.
Work 1 row.
Bind off rem 9(11:13) sts.
With right side facing, rejoin yarn to rem 34(36:38) sts, bind off 5 sts, patt to end.
Patt 1 row.
Bind off 5 sts at beg of next row and 3 foll right side rows.
Work 1 row.
Bind off rem 9(11:13) sts.

Front edging

With right sides together, fold hood in half and join shaped bound-off edge.
With right side facing and size US 5 circular needle, pick up and k98(104:110) sts up right side of opening to top hood seam, then 97(103:109) sts down left side of front opening. *195(207:219) sts*
Work backward and forward in rows.
1st row: P2, [k2, p2] to last 5 sts, k2, p3.
2nd row: K3, [p2, k2] to end.
These 2 rows form the rib and are repeated.
Work a further 25(27:29) rows in rib.
Bind off in rib.

To make up

Sew row ends of right front edging to bound-off edge at center front.
Sew row ends of left side to back of seam.
With center of bound-off edge of sleeves to shoulder seam, sew on sleeves.
Leaving row ends open at lower edge, join side and sleeve seams, reversing seams for cuff.
Weave in all ends.

PONCHO

To introduce you to cables for the first time, I have placed them on a garment with no shaping so that you can concentrate on the technique. Two strips sewn together form the poncho, which is an ideal garment to slip easily over a baby's or child's head, and on a really chilly day is roomy enough to add warmth over a coat. The four-stitch cable is easier than it looks—you are just holding two stitches while you are knitting another two.

Measurements

To fit ages

6–12	12–18	18–24	months

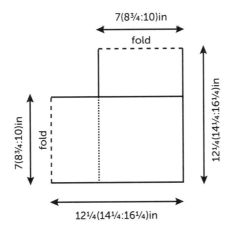

7(8¾:10)in

fold

fold

7(8¾:10)in

fold

12¼(14¼:16¼)in

12¼(14¼:16¼)in

Materials

3(3:4) x 1¾oz (50g) balls of Debbie Bliss Cashmerino Aran in Silver 202
Pair of size US 8 knitting needles
Cable needle

Gauge

23 sts and 26 rows to 4in square over cable patt using size US 8 needles

Abbreviations

C4B   cable four stitches back: slip next 2 sts onto a cable needle and hold at back of work, k2, then k2 from cable needle (page 112)

Also see page 19

THE PATTERN

Panel

(Make 2)

With size US 8 needles, cast on 42(50:58) sts.

1st row: P3, [k4, p4] 4(5:6) times, k4, p3.

2nd row: P to end.

3rd row: P3, [C4B, p4] 4(5:6) times, k4, p3.

Cable back (see right)

4th row: P to end.

These 4 rows form the cable patt and are repeated 26(29:32) times more.

Bind off.

To make up

Join cast-on edge of second piece to right-hand side of first piece along row ends of first 48(56:64) rows. Join bound-off edge of first piece to left-hand side of second piece along row ends of last 48(56:64) rows.

Weave in all ends.

THE TECHNIQUES

Cable back

This cable has stitches held at the back of the work on a cable needle while the next stitches on the left-hand needle are worked, followed by those on the cable needle; the cable twists to the right. The example shown is over four stitches and would be abbreviated to "C4B" in a knitting pattern. Fewer or more stitches can be used, but with a bulkier yarn using too many stitches should be avoided.

2 Move the cable needle and the stitches on it to the back of the work, then knit the next two stitches from the left-handle needle.

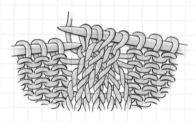

3 Then knit the two stitches from the cable needle to complete the cable.

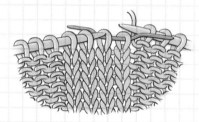

1 Work to the position of the cable. Slip the next two stitches from the left-hand needle onto the cable needle.

VEST

This classic knitted vest lets you explore the world of cables further. There are three cable styles featured, but all use the same simple technique of holding some stitches while others are worked. The tank top has a classic crew neck, but with a back opening to make sure it slips easily over a child's head.

Measurements

To fit ages

0–3	3–6	6–9	9–12	12–18	18–24	months

Finished measurements

Chest

17¾	19¼	20¾	22½	24	25½	in

Length to shoulder

8¾	9½	10¼	11	12½	14¼	in

Materials

2(2:3:3:3:4) 1¾oz (50g) x balls of Debbie Bliss Baby Cashmerino in Mink 64
Pair each of size US 2 and 3 knitting needles
Size US 2 or 3 short circular needle (see my note on page 49)
Cable needle *Pattern note: Cable needle (page 116)*
1 small button

Gauge

25 sts and 34 rows to 4in square over st st using size US 3 needles

Pattern note: Cable needle

Using a cranked or hooked cable needle, rather than a straight cable needle, can be easier if you are new to cabling, as it's almost impossible for the stitches to fall off while you are working the cable.

Abbreviations

C2B   cable two stitches back: slip next stitch onto cable needle and hold at back of work, k1, then k1 from cable needle

C2F   cable two stitches front: slip next stitch onto cable needle and hold to front of work, k1, then k1 from cable needle

C4B   cable four stitches back: slip next 2 stitches onto cable needle and hold at back of work, k2, then k2 from cable needle

C4F   cable four stitches front: slip next 2 stitches onto cable needle and hold to front of work, k2, then k2 from cable needle (page 120)

C6B   cable six stitches back: slip next 3 stitches onto cable needle and hold at back of work, k3, then k3 from cable needle

C6F   cable six stitches front: slip next 3 stitches onto cable needle and hold to front of work, k3, then k3 from cable needle

m1pw   make one stitch purlwise: pick up and purl into back of loop lying between stitch just worked and next st (page 121)

p2tog tbl purl two stitches together through the back loops (page 121)

yon   yarn over needle

Also see page 19

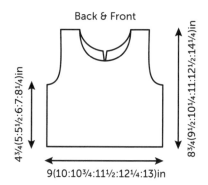

Back & Front

4¾(5:5½:6:7:8¼)in

8¾(9½:10¼:11:12½:14¼)in

9(10:10¾:11½:12¼:13)in

THE PATTERN

Back

With size US 2 or 3 needles, cast on 60(66:72:78:84:90) sts.

1st row (wrong side): P2(5:2:5:2:5), [k4, p2] 2(2:3:3:4:4) times, k4, [p3, k4] 3 times, p3, k4, [p2, k4] 2(2:3:3:4:4) times, p2(5:2:5:2:5).

2nd row: K2(5:2:5:2:5), [p4, C2F] 2(2:3:3:4:4) times, p4, [k3, p4] 3 times, k3, p4, [C2B, p4] 2(2:3:3:4:4) times, k2(5:2:5:2:5).

Cable front (page 120)

Rep the last 2 rows twice more.

Inc row (wrong side): Patt 20(23:26:29:32:35), [m1pw, patt 7] 3 times, m1pw, patt 19(22:25:28:31:34). *64(70:76:82:88:94) sts*

Make one purlwise (page 121)

Change to size US 3 needles. Now work in patt as follows:

1st row (right side): P6(9:6:9:6:9), [C2F, p4] 2(2:3:3:4:4) times, k4, p4, k12, p4, k4, [p4, C2B] 2(2:3:3:4:4) times, p6(9:6:9:6:9).

2nd row: K6(9:6:9:6:9), [p2, k4] 2(2:3:3:4:4) times, p4, k4, p12, k4, p4, [k4, p2] 2(2:3:3:4:4) times, k6(9:6:9:6:9).

3rd and 4th rows: As 1st and 2nd rows.

5th row: P6(9:6:9:6:9), [C2F, p4] 2(2:3:3:4:4) times, C4F, p4, C6B, C6F, p4, C4B, [p4, C2B] 2(2:3:3:4:4) times, p6(9:6:9:6:9).

Pattern note: Other cable patterns (see right)

6th row: K6(9:6:9:6:9), [p2, k4] 2(2:3:3:4:4) times, p4, k4, p12, k4, p4, [k4, p2] 2(2:3:3:4:4) times, k6(9:6:9:6:9).

These 6 rows form the patt and are repeated.

Cont in patt and work until back measures 4¾(5:5½:6:7:8¼)in from cast-on edge, ending with a wrong side row.

Shape armholes

Bind off 4(5:5:6:6:7) sts at beg of next 2 rows. *56(60:66:70:76:80) sts*

Next row and 2(2:3:3:4:4) foll right side rows: Skpo, patt to last 2 sts, k2tog. *50(54:58:62:66:70) sts ***

Cont in patt until back measures 6(6¾:7½:8¼:10:11½)in from cast-on edge, ending with a wrong side row.

Back neck opening

1st row (right side): Patt 25(27:29:31:33:35) sts, turn and work on these sts only for first side of neck shaping, leave rem sts on a spare needle.

2nd row: Cast on 1 st, then work k1, patt to end. *26(28:30:32:34:36) sts*

Next row: Patt to last st, k1.

Next row: K1, patt to end.

Rep the last 2 rows until back measures 8(8¾:9½:10¼:12:13¼)in from cast-on edge, ending with a wrong side row.

Pattern note: Other cable patterns

Don't be put off by what seems to be a more complex center cable—all cables are worked on the same simple technique of holding some stitches while working others. This cable is formed from placing the two four-stitch cables together to form a larger one. The two-stitch cable on the sides is simplicity itself.

Shape neck

Next row: Patt 16(17:18:19:20:21) sts, turn, leave rem 10(11:12:13:14:15) sts on a safety pin.

Next row: P2tog, patt to end.

Next row: Patt to last 2 sts, k2tog. Rep the last 2 rows once more. *12(13:14:15:16:17) sts*

Work 3 rows in patt.

Bind off for shoulder.

With right side facing, pick up and k 1 st from base of last st on first side of back opening, patt to end. *26(28:30:32:34:36) sts*

Next row: Patt to last st, k1.

Next row: K1, patt to end. Rep the last 2 rows until back measures 8(8¾:9½:10¼:12:13¼)in from cast-on edge, ending with a wrong side row.

Shape neck

Next row: Decreasing 2 sts over the 4-st cable, patt 10(11:12:13:14:15) sts, leave these 8(9:10:11:12:13) sts on a safety pin, patt to end. *16(17:18:19:20:21) sts*

Pattern note: Decreasing two stitches over a cable (page 120)

Next row: Patt to last 2 sts, p2tog tbl.

Purl two together through back loops (page 121)

Next row: Skpo, patt to end. Rep the last 2 rows once more. *12(13:14:15:16:17) sts*

Work 3 rows in patt.

Bind off for shoulder.

Front

Work as given for back to **.

Cont in patt until front measures 6¼(7:8:8¾:10:11½)in from cast-on edge, ending with a wrong side row.

Shape neck

Next row (right side): Patt 19(20:21:22:23:24) sts, turn and work on these sts only for first side of front neck, leave rem sts on a spare needle.

Next row: Bind off 2, patt to end.

Patt 1 row.

Rep the last 2 rows once more. *15(16:17:18:19:20) sts*

Next row: P2tog, patt to end.

Patt 1 row.

Rep the last 2 rows twice more. *12(13:14:15:16:17) sts*

Work straight until front measures same as back to shoulder, ending with a wrong side row.

Bind off for shoulder.

With right side facing, rejoin yarn to rem sts, then decreasing 2 sts over each 6-st cable, patt center 12(14:16:18:20:22) sts, slip these 8(10:12:14:16:18) sts onto a holder, patt to end. *19(20:21:22:23:24) sts*

Next row: Patt to end.

Next row: Bind off 2, patt to end.

Rep the last 2 rows once more. *15(16:17:18:19:20) sts*

Next row: Patt to end.

Next row: P2tog, patt to end. Rep the last 2 rows twice more. *12(13:14:15:16:17) sts*

Work straight until front measures same as back to shoulder, ending with a wrong side row.

Bind off for shoulder.

Neckband

Join shoulder seams.

With right side facing and size US 2 or 3 circular needle, slip 8(9:10:11:12:13) sts from left back safety pin onto the needle, pick up and k7 sts up left back neck, 23(23:23:23:25:25) sts down left front neck, k across 8(10:12:14:16:18) sts from front neck holder, pick up and k23(23:23:23:25:25) sts up right front neck, 7 sts down right back neck, then decreasing 2 sts over the 4-st cable, patt 10(11:12:13:14:15) sts from back neck holder, then cast on 2 sts. *86(90:94:98:106:110) sts*

1st row (wrong side): K3, [p2, k2] to last 3 sts, p2, k1.

2nd row: K3, [p2, k2] to last 7 sts, p2, k5.

3rd (buttonhole) row: K3, p2, [k2, p2] to last 3 sts, p2tog, yon, k1.

4th row: Rib to end.

Bind off in patt.

Armbands

With right side facing and size US 2 or 3 needles, pick up and k66(70:78:82:90:94) sts around armhole edge.

1st row (wrong side): P2, [k2, p2] to end.

2nd row: K2, [p2, k2] to end. These 2 rows form the rib and are repeated once more.

Bind off in rib.

To make up

Join side and armband seams.

Weave in all ends.

Sew on button.

THE TECHNIQUES

Pattern note: Decreasing two stitches over a cable

Cables on seams can create an uneven or lumpy appearance, which is particularly noticeable on shoulder seams. This effect can be lessened by decreasing sts across a cable as you bind off. On this project the 2-stitch cables at the shoulder are too small to distort the fabric so decreasing those isn't necessary, but in order to make a smooth transition from the center cable to the neckband, decreasing is used on the center cable as the front neck stitches are bound off. To do this, work in pattern to the position of the cable, then work skpo (page 54) over the first two stitches of the cable group, then k2tog (page 54) over the last two stitches.

Cable front

This cable has stitches held at the front of the work on a cable needle while the next stitches on the left-hand needle are worked, followed by those on the cable needle; the cable twists to the left. The example shown here is over four stitches and would be abbreviated to "C4F" in a knitting pattern, but fewer or more stitches can be used. This technique produces a cable that looks like a rope—if you use a cable front followed by a cable back, a "snake" will be formed.

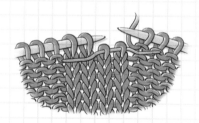

1 Work to the position of the cable. Slip the next two stitches from the left-hand needle onto the cable needle.

2 Bring the cable needle and the stitches on it to the front of the work, then knit the next two stitches from the left-hand needle.

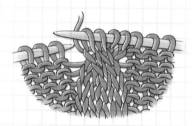

3 Then knit the two stitches from the cable needle to complete the cable.

Make one purlwise

This increase is usually abbreviated to "m1pw". It slopes to the left on stockinette stitch (to the right on reverse stockinette stitch). In order to avoid making a small hole, purl into the back of the raised strand.

2 Insert the right-hand needle purlwise into the back of the loop formed by the strand.

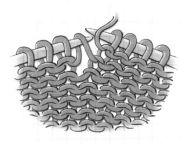

1 From the front, slip the tip of the left-hand needle under the horizontal strand of yarn lying between the last stitch on the right-hand needle and the first stitch on the left-hand needle.

3 Purl the loop as if it were a stitch. You have increased by one stitch.

Purl two together through back loops

This is usually abbreviated to "p2tog tbl". This decrease slants to the left on stockinette stitch (the right on reverse stockinette stitch).

1 From left to right, insert the right-hand needle into the next two stitches on the left-hand needle, as shown. This can be tricky if your gauge is tight: try inserting the needle through the stitches purlwise first, and gently stretching them.

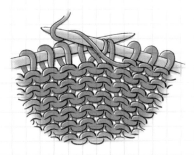

2 Purl the two stitches together as one, as for p2tog (page 70). You have decreased by one stitch.

CROSSOVER TOP

A ballerina-style top has the advantage of being not only attractive but also really practical. On a small baby the tie fastening can be a lot easier to achieve than trying to do up tiny buttons on a cardigan, especially when you are in a hurry. A lace edge, such as the one I have used here, adds a bit more decorative detail to a simple top.

Measurements

To fit ages

3–6	6–9	9–12	12–18	18–24	months

Finished measurements

Chest

20	21¼	22	2½	25¼	in

Length to shoulder

8¾	9½	10¾	12	12½	in

Sleeve length

5½	6	6¾	7½	8¾	in

Materials

3(3:4:4:5) x 1¾oz (50g) balls of Debbie Bliss Baby Cashmerino in Light Pink 600
Pair each of size US 2 and size US 3 knitting needles

Gauge

25 sts and 34 rows to 4in square over st st using size US 3 needles

Abbreviations

See page 19

Back & Fronts

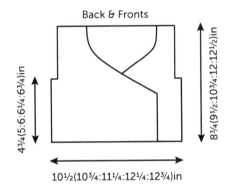

8¾(9½:10¾:12:12½)in

4¾(5:6:6¼:6¾)in

10½(10¾:11¼:12¼:12¾)in

Sleeves

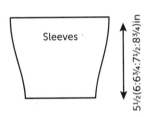

5½(6:6¾:7½:8¾)in

THE PATTERN

Back

With size US 2 needles, cast on
66(69:72:77:82) sts.
K 3 rows.
Change to size US 3 needles.
Beg with a k row, work
38(42:48:54:60) rows in st st.
Shape armholes
Bind off 4 sts at beg of next
2 rows. *58(61:64:69:74) sts*
Work a further 32(36:40:44:48)
rows.
Shape shoulders
Bind off 14(15:16:18:20) sts at beg
of next 2 rows.
Bind off rem 30(31:32:33:34) sts.

Left front

With size US 2 needles, cast on
56(59:62:66:70) sts.
K 3 rows.
Change to size US 3 needles.
1st row (right side): K to end.
2nd row: K4, p to end.
Rep the last 2 rows 12(14:17:20:23)
times more.
Shape front slope
Next row: K to end.
Next row: Bind off 4 sts,
p to end.
Next row: K to last 3 sts, k2tog, k1.
Next row: P1, p2tog, p to end.
Rep the last 2 rows 4 times more.
42(45:48:52:56) sts
Shape armhole
Next row: Bind off 4 sts, k to last
3 sts, k2tog, k1.
Next row: P1, p2tog, p to end.
Next row: K to last 3 sts, k2tog, k1.
Next row: P1, p2tog, p to end.
Rep the last 2 rows 10(11:12:13:14)

times more. *14(15:16:18:20) sts*
Work 10(12:14:16:18) rows, ending
with a p row.
Shape shoulder
Next row: Bind off.

Right front

With size US 2 needles, cast on
56(59:62:66:70) sts.
K 3 rows.
Change to size US 3 needles.
1st row: K to end.
2nd row: P to last 4 sts, k4.
Rep the last 2 rows 12(14:17:20:23)
times more.
Shape front slope
Next row: Bind off 4 sts, k to end.
Next row: P to end.
Next row: K1, skpo, k to end.
Next row: P to last 3 sts,
p2tog tbl, p1.
Rep the last 2 rows 4 times more.
42(45:48:52:56) sts
Next row: K1, skpo, k to end.
Shape armhole
Next row: Bind off 4 sts, p to last 3
sts, p2tog tbl, p1.
Next row: K1, skpo, k to end.
Next row: P to last 3 sts,
p2tog tbl, p1.
Rep the last 2 rows 10(11:12:13:14)
times more. *14(15:16:18:20) sts*
Work 11(13:15:17:19) rows, ending
with a p row.
Shape shoulder
Next row: Bind off.

Sleeves

With size US 2 needles, cast on
38(42:46:50:52) sts.
K 3 rows.
Change to size US 3 needles.
Beg with a k row, work in st st.
Work 6 rows.
Inc row: K3, m1, k to last 3 sts,
m1, k3.
Work 3 rows.
Rep the last 4 rows 4(5:6:7:8)
times more and the inc row again.
50(56:62:68:72) sts
Cont straight until sleeve
measures 5½(6:6¾:7½:8¾)in from
cast-on edge, ending with a p row.
Place a marker at each end of
last row.
Work a further 6 rows.
Bind off.

Neck edging

With size US 3 needles, cast on 3 sts.
1st row: K2, yf, k to end.
2nd row: K to end.
3rd to 9th rows: Rep 1st and 2nd
rows 3 times and the 1st row again.
8 sts
8th row: Bind off 5 sts, k to end.
3 sts
Rep 1st to 10th rows until border fits
around neck edge, ending with a
10th row.
Bind off.

THE TECHNIQUES

Sewing on lace

If the gauges are reasonably compatible, the neatest way to sew on a lace trim is with mattress stitch (page 83). Here, the straight edge of the lace is being sewn to the shaped edge of the plain knitted fabric, but you can also easily sew row ends (the top edge of lace that's knitted lengthways) to a cast-on edge. If the gauges of the trim and the main knitting are not at all similar, then sew the lace on with backstitch or oversewing.

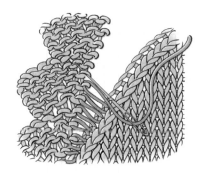

Right tie
With size US 2 needles, cast on 5 sts.
Work in garter st for 6¼in.
Bind off.

Left tie
With size US 2 needles, cast on 5 sts.
Work in garter st for
19(19¾:20½:21¼:22)in.
Bind off.

To make up
Join shoulder seams. With center of bound-off edge of sleeve to shoulder seam, sew sleeves into armholes, easing to fit and with row ends above markers sewn to sts bound off at underarm.
Leaving a small opening in right side seam level with beg of neck shaping, join sleeve and side seams.
Sew neck edging in place.
Sewing on lace (see left)
Sew ties to fronts at beg and end of edging.
Weave in all ends.

STRIPED
SWEATER

There are few things I like better than a Breton top, whether on myself or a baby! Simple stripes are a great way to start using color as the technique is easy to master. The square neck and button fastening on the shoulder of this sweater make it easy to slip over a baby's head (you may have started to notice that ease over a head figures largely in my design briefs!), and I have introduced a contrast shade on neckband and cuffs to add more color.

Measurements

To fit ages

3-6	6-9	9-12	12-18	18-24	months

Finished measurements

Chest

20	22	24	25½	27½	in

Length to shoulder

10¼	11	12¼	13½	14½	in

Sleeve length

5½	6	6¾	7½	8¾	in

Materials

2(2:3:3:3:4) x 1¾oz (50g) balls of Debbie Bliss Baby Cashmerino in Ecru 101 (M), 1(1:1:2:2:2) x 1¾oz (50g) balls in Duck Egg 026 (A) and 1 x 1¾oz (50g) ball in Wasabi 313 (B)
Pair each of size US 2 and size US 3 knitting needles
4 buttons

Gauge

25 sts and 34 rows to 4in square over st st using size US 3 needles

Abbreviations

See page 19

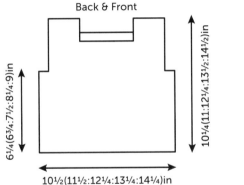

Back & Front

6¼(6¾:7½:8¼:9)in

10½(11½:12¼:13¼:14¼)in

10¼(11:12¼:13½:14½)in

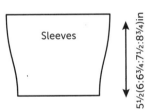

Sleeves

5½(6:6¾:7½:8¾)in

THE PATTERN

Back

With size US 2 needles and M,
cast on 66(72:78:84:90) sts.
K 7 rows.
Change to size US 3 needles.
Next row (right side): K to end.
Next row: K3, p to last 3 sts, k3.
Rep the last 2 rows 1(1:2:2:3) times
more.
Beg with a k row, work in st st and
stripes of 2 rows A, [2 rows M, 2
rows A] twice, 4 rows M until back
measures 6¼(6½:7½:8¼:9)in from
cast-on edge, ending with a k row.
Joining in a new color (page 133)
Carrying yarn up the side of the
work (page 133)
Shape armholes
Next row (wrong side): Bind off
4 sts, p to last 4 sts, bind off these
4 sts. *58(64:70:76:82) sts*
Break off yarns.
With right side facing, rejoin
correct color yarn to cont the stripe
sequence and work straight in
st st until back measures
9(10:11:12¼:13½)in from
cast-on edge, ending with a p row.
Shape shoulders and back neck
Next row (right side):
K14(16:19:21:24) sts, turn and
work on these sts only for first side
of back neck, leave rem sts on a
spare needle.
Work 7 rows in striped st st, ending
with a p row.

Change to size US 2 needles.
With M, k 3 rows.
Bind off knitwise on
wrong side.
With right side facing, slip center
30(30:32:32:34) sts onto a holder,
rejoin yarn to rem sts, k to end.
Work 7 rows striped st st, ending
with a p row.
Change to size US 2 needles.
With M, k 3 rows.
Bind off knitwise on wrong side.
Back neckband
With right side facing, size US
2 needles, and B, pick up and
k8 sts down right back neck,
k30(30:32:32:34) sts from back neck
holder, then pick up and k8 sts up
left back neck. *46(46:48:48:50) sts*
K 1 row.
Dec row: K6, skpo, k2tog,
k26(26:28:28:30), skpo, k2tog, k6.
K 1 row.
Dec row: K5, skpo, k2tog,
k24(24:26:26:28), skpo, k2tog, k5.
Bind off knitwise on wrong side.

Front

Work as given for back until 6 rows fewer have been worked than on back to start of neck shaping, ending with a p row.

Shape shoulders and front neck

Next row (right side): K14(16:19:21:24), turn and work on these sts only for first side of front neck, leave rem sts on a spare needle.

Work 13 rows in st st, ending with a p row.

Change to size US 2 needles.

K 1 row.

Buttonhole row: K8(9:10:11:12), yf, k2tog, k to end.

K 1 row.

Bind off knitwise on wrong side.

With right side facing, slip center 30(30:32:32:34) sts onto a holder, rejoin yarn to rem sts, k to end.

Work 13 rows in st st, ending with a p row.

Change to size US 2 needles.

K 1 row.

Buttonhole row: K8(10:12:14:16), yf, k2tog, k to end.

K 1 row.

Bind off knitwise on wrong side.

Front neckband

With right side facing, size US 2 needles, and B, pick up and k13 sts down right front neck, k30(30:32:32:34) sts from front neck holder, then pick up and k13 sts up left front neck. *56(56:58:60) sts*

K 1 row.

Dec (buttonhole) row: K2, yf, k2tog, k7, skpo, k2tog, k26(26:28:28:30), skpo, k2tog, k7, k2tog, yf, k2.

K 1 row.

Dec row: K10, skpo, k2tog, k24(24:26:26:28), skpo, k2tog, k10.

Bind off knitwise on wrong side.

Sleeves

With size US 2 needles and B, cast on 42(46:46:50:54) sts.

1st row: K2, [p2, k2] to end.

2nd row: P2, [k2, p2] to end.

Rep the last 2 rows 4(5:5:6:6) times more.

Change to size US 3 needles.

Working in stripe sequence of 4 rows M, 2 rows A, [2 rows M, 2 rows A] twice throughout, work as follows:

Beg with a k row, work 6 rows in st st.

Inc row: K3, m1, k to last 3 sts, m1, k3.

Work 5 rows in st st.

Rep the last 6 rows 3(3:5:5:6) times more and the inc row again. *52(56:60:64:70) sts*

Cont straight until sleeve measures 5½(6:6¾:7½:8¾)in from cast on edge, ending with a p row.

Place a marker at each end of last row.

Work a further 6 rows.

Bind off.

To make up

Lap buttonhole bands over button bands and baste in place at side edges.

With center of bound-off edge of sleeve to shoulder, sew sleeves into armholes, easing to fit, and with row ends above markers sewn to sts bound off at underarm.

Join sleeve and side seams to top of garter st opening.

Weave in all ends.

Sew on buttons.

THE TECHNIQUES

Joining in a new color

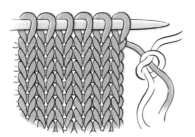

1 To join in the new yarn, tie the free end around the tail of the old yarn in a single knot.

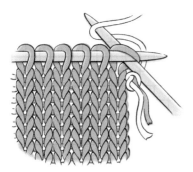

2 Slip the knot up the tail of the old yarn until it is tight against the knitting, then start the row using the new yarn. When you have completed the knitting, you can unpick the knot (if need be) and sew the ends in (page 149).

Carrying yarn up the side of the work

In repeat stripe patterns you do not need to join in a new color for every stripe. Instead you can carry the colors not in use up the side of the work. The loops created by doing this will be sewn into the seams, although short loops look tidy enough on unseamed edges, such as the edges of a scarf.

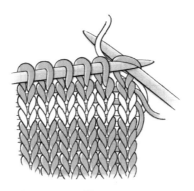

1 If you are working a two-row stripe, then just knit the first stitch of the row after it with the previous color.

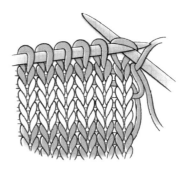

2 If the stripes are wider stripes, catch in the yarn being carried up the side at the start of every third row. Put the right-hand needle into the first stitch, lay the yarn to be carried over the working yarn, and work the stitch in the working yarn.

FAIR ISLE

SWEATER

Fair Isle patterning is one of my greatest loves. However, an all-over pattern when you are just starting this color technique can be rather overwhelming, so I have introduced it in a panel across the body and left the rest plain. There are side vents to make the sweater easier to go over a bulky diaper, and a back button fastening.

Measurements

To fit ages

3–6	6–9	9–12	12–18	18–24	months

Finished measurements

Chest

19¾	21¾	23½	25½	27½	in

Length to back neck

9½	10¼	11	12¼	13¾	in

Sleeve length

5½	6	6¾	7½	8¾	in

Materials

3(3:4:4:5) x 1¾oz (50g) balls of Debbie Bliss Baby Cashmerino in Camel 102 (M)
Small amount of Chocolate 11 (A), Denim 27 (B), Ecru 101 (C), Rose Pink 94 (D) and Red 34 (E)
Pair each of size US 2 and 3 knitting needles (see my note on page 49)
Short 3 size US 3 circular needle
2 small buttons

Gauge

25 sts and 34 rows to 4in square over st st using size US 3 needles

Abbreviations

See page 19

Chart notes

Pattern note: Working a charted pattern (page 136)
Vertical lines on the chart indicate the 8-st patt repeat and also the sts to be worked at either side of the repeat, for each size—take care to use the lines for your chosen size. Carry yarns not in use across the wrong side of the work, weaving the stranded yarn in where it crosses more than 3 sts.
Pattern note: Stranding (page 140)

Pattern note: Working a charted pattern

Color motifs or designs are often given as charts within a written pattern. Sometimes the instructions are written out as well, but usually the written instructions will tell you how to place the chart on the knitting and then how much of the chart to knit, or if it is a repeat section of a stranded or a slip stitch pattern, how often you should repeat it. Charts have an advantage over words in that you can see what the pattern you are producing should look like, and it is simple to spot any mistakes early on.

In a chart a single block represents one stitch, so a horizontal line of blocks is one row. Colors will be shown either with colored blocks or symbols, and the chart will have a key that tells you what each colored block or symbol represents.

The first row of the chart is the bottom one, and you will usually start a chart on a right-side row in the knitting—as here—so the first stitch you knit from the chart will be the bottom right-hand one. When knitting back and forth, the right-side rows are read from right to left, and wrong-side rows from left to right.

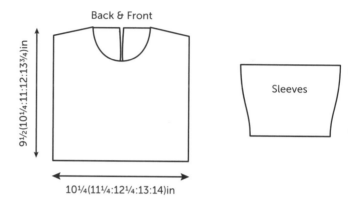

Back & Front

9½(10¼:11:12:13¾)in

10¼(11¼:12¼:13:14)in

Sleeves

5½(6¼:6¾:7½:8¾)in

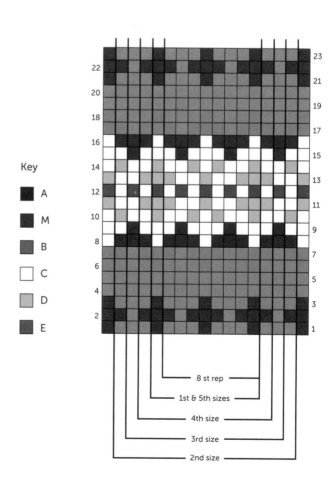

Key

A

M

B

C

D

E

8 st rep

1st & 5th sizes

4th size

3rd size

2nd size

THE PATTERN

Back

With size US 2 or 3 needles and M, cast on 64(72:76:84:88) sts.

1st rib row: K5, [p2, k2] to last 7 sts, p2, k5.

2nd rib row: K3, [p2, k2] to last 5 sts, p2, k3.

Rep the last 2 rows 4(4:5:5:6) times and the 1st row again.

Next row: Rib to end and inc(dec:inc:dec:inc) 1 st at center of row. 65(71:77:83:89) sts

Change to size US 3 needles.

Beg with a k row, work 28(34:38:48:58) rows in st st.

Place Fair Isle chart

Joining in a new color (page 140)
Holding one yarn at a time (page 141)

1st row: K0(3:2:1:0) sts before patt rep, k across 8-st patt rep 8(8:9:10:11) times, then k1(4:3:2:1) sts after patt rep.

2nd row: P1(4:3:2:1) sts before patt rep, p across 8-st patt rep 8(8:9:10:11) times, then p0(3:2:1:0) sts after patt rep.

These 2 rows set the position for the Fair Isle chart.

Cont to work from the chart until the 23rd chart row has been worked. Cont in M only and beg with a p row, work 3(3:5:5:7) rows **.

Divide for back opening

1st row (right side):
K30(33:36:39:42), turn, cast on 5 sts and cont on these 35(38:41:44:47) sts only, leave rem sts on a spare needle.

2nd row: K5, p to end.

3rd row: K to end.

4th to 10th rows: Rep 2nd and 3rd rows 3 times more, then the 2nd row again.

Shape shoulder

Bind off 6(7:8:9:10) sts at beg of next row and foll right side row.

Next row: K5, p to end.

Next row: Bind off 6 sts, k to end.

Next row: K5, p to end.

Leave rem 17(18:19:20:21) sts on a holder for back neck.

With right side facing, rejoin yarn to rem sts and work as follows:

1st row: K to end.

2nd row: P to last 5 sts, k5.

3rd to 10th rows: Rep 1st and 2nd rows 4 times more.

11th (buttonhole) row: K2, k2tog, yf, k to end.

Shape shoulder

Bind off 6(7:8:9:10) sts at beg of next row and foll wrong side row.

Next row: K to end.

Next row: Bind off 6 sts, p to last 5 sts, k5.

Leave rem 17(18:19:20:21) sts on a spare needle for back neck, do not break off yarn, leave the work to one side.

Front

Work as given for back to **.

Shape front neck

1st row: K20(22:24:26:28), k2tog, k2, turn and work on these sts only for first side of neck, leave rem sts on a spare needle.

2nd row: P2, p2tog, p to end.

3rd row: K to last 4 sts, k2tog, k2.

4th to 6th rows: Rep 2nd and 3rd rows once and the 2nd row again. *18(20:22:24:26) sts*

Work 4 rows straight.

Shape shoulder

Bind off 6(7:8:9:10) sts at beg of next row and foll right side row.

Next row: P to end.

Next row: Bind off 6 rem sts.

With right side facing, slip center 17(19:21:23:25) sts onto a holder, rejoin yarn to rem sts.

1st row: K2, skpo, k to end.

2nd row: P to last 4 sts, p2tog tbl, p2.

4th to 6th rows: Rep 1st and 2nd rows twice more. *18(20:22:24:26) sts*

Work 5 rows straight.

Shape shoulder

Bind off 6(7:8:9:10) sts at beg of next row and foll wrong side row.

Next row: K to end.

Next row: Bind off 6 rem sts.

Neckband

Join shoulder seams.

With right side facing, size US 3 circular needle, and M, k across 17(18:19:20:21) sts from left back holder, pick up and k12 sts down left front neck, k across 17(19:21:23:25) sts on front neck holder, pick up and k13 sts up right front neck, then k across 17(18:19:20:21) sts from right back holder. *76(80:84:88:92) sts*

Work backward and forward in rows, not rounds.

1st rib row: K5, [p2, k2] to last 7 sts, p2, k5.

2nd rib row: K7, [p2, k2] to last 9 sts, p2, k7.

3rd rib row: As 1st rib row.

4th rib (buttonhole) row: K2, k2tog, yf, k3, [p2, k2] to last 9 sts, p2, k7.

5th to 7th rows: Rep 1st and 2nd rows once and 1st row again.

Bind off in patt.

Sleeves

(Make 2)

With size US 2 or 3 needles and M, cast on 42(46:46:50:54) sts.

1st row: K2, [p2, k2] to end.

2nd row: P2, [k2, p2] to end.

Rep the last 2 rows 4(5:5:6:6) times more.

Change to size US 3 needles.

Beg with a k row, work in st st as follows:

Work 6 rows.

Inc row: K3, m1, k to last 3 sts, m1, k3.

Work 5 rows.

Rep the last 6 rows 3(3:5:5:6) times more and the inc row again. *52(56:60:64:70) sts*

Cont straight until sleeve measures 5½(6:6¾:7½:8¾)in from cast-on edge, ending with a p row.

Bind off.

To make up

Lap buttonhole band over button band and stitch the 5 cast-on sts of button band behind the lower edge of buttonhole band.

With center of bound-off edge of sleeve to shoulder, sew on sleeves.

Join sleeve seam and side seams to top of garter st opening.

Weave in all ends.

Sew on buttons.

Pattern note: Stranding

This is the technique to use for a color pattern that is repeated across the knitting. The color of yarn that is not making stitches is stranded across the back of the knitting until it is needed next, and correctly tensioning these loose strands, which are called "floats," is key to working the technique well. It is important that the floats are not pulled too tightly to ensure that the fabric remains elastic and the stitches aren't distorted. You should strand the yarns right across the back of the knitting, from edge stitch to edge stitch—even if the final stitch in a given color is several stitches in from an edge—or the last stitches in a given color will pull and distort. You should aim for the Fair Isle band on the sweater to be the same width as the plain stockinette stitch sections.

Joining in a new color

New yarns are usually joined in at the start of a row (page 36 and 133), and carried right across the fabric, but sometimes you may have to join in a yarn in the middle of a row if only a section is being stranded.

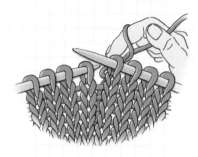

1 On a knit row, work to the color change. Lay the new color over the existing color, with the working yarn to the right and a tail about 4in long to the left. Make a single twist to take the new color under the old color, as shown.

2 Knit the stitch with the new color. Knit a few more stitches, then pull gently on the tail to tighten up the first stitch in the new color. Sew in the tail when the knitting is complete.

3 On a purl row, work to the color change. Lay the new color over the existing color, with the working yarn to the right and a tail about 4in long to the left. Twist the two yarns together with a single twist, as shown.

4 Purl the stitch with the new color. Purl a few more stitches, then pull gently on the tail to tighten up the first stitch in the new color. Sew in the tail when the knitting is complete.

Holding one yarn at a time

This is the least efficient method of managing the yarns, but is usually the easiest for beginners. The technique is simple enough, it's getting the tension right that takes practice. The float (the strand of the second color yarn coming across the back of the first color stitches) should lie flat against the back of the knitting without being stretched, or it will pull the fabric in.

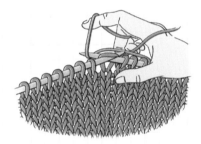

1 On a knit row, knit the stitches in color A (brown in this example), bringing it across over the strand of color B (blue in this example) to wrap around the needle.

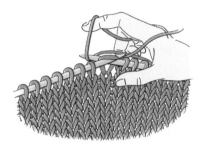

2 At the color change, drop color A and pick up color B, bringing it across under the strand of color A to wrap around the needle, and making sure not to pull it too tight. Knit the stitches in color B. When you change back to color A, bring it across over the strand of color B.

3 On a purl row, purl the stitches in color A (brown in this example), bringing it across over the strand of color B (blue in this example) to wrap around the needle.

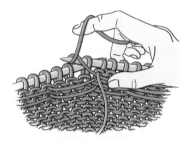

4 At the color change, drop color A and pick up color B, bringing it across under the strand of color A to wrap around the needle, and making sure not to pull it too tight. Purl the stitches in color B. When you change back to color A, bring it across over the strand of color B. You can clearly see how the strands interlace at the back of the work; color A (blue) always comes across over color B (brown), and color B always comes across under color A.

INTARSIA
SWEATER

This sweater has a relatively easy motif to knit that is just composed of circles. The technique used is the intarsia method, using different lengths of yarn rather than stranding the yarn so as to keep the motifs as flat as possible. The sweater has side vents, shoulder fastenings, dropped shoulders, and a square neck front and back.

Measurements
To fit ages

3–6	6–9	9–12	12–18	18–24	months

Finished measurements

Chest

19¾	21¾	23½	25½	27½	in

Length to shoulder

10¼	11	12	13½	15	in

Sleeve length

6	6¾	7½	8¼	9½	in

Materials
3(3:3:4:4) x 1¾oz (50g) balls of Debbie Bliss Baby Cashmerino in Silver 12 (A) and 1 x 1¾oz (50g) ball in each of Mink 64 (B) and Chocolate 11 (C)
Pair each of size US 2 and 3 knitting needles (see my note on page 49)
4 small buttons

Gauge
25 sts and 34 rows to 4in square over st st using size US 3 needles

Abbreviations
See page 19

Chart notes
Pattern note: Intarsia (page 144)
Work from chart, using separate small balls of yarn for each color area.
You could Swiss darn the eyes on completion instead of knitting them in.
Swiss darning (page 146)

Pattern note: Intarsia

Intarsia is used for larger blocks of color rather than for all-over Fair Isle patterns. To keep the pattern or motif as flat as possible, a separate ball or length of yarn is used for each area of color, twisting the yarns on the wrong side at the color change to avoid holes forming between the two colors. I prefer to work with shortish lengths because it is difficult to stop the balls twisting round each other and tangling up—with lengths you can pull them through if they get into a knot.

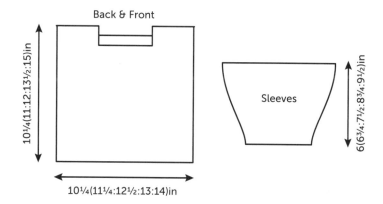

Back & Front

10¼(11:12:13½:15)in

10¼(11¼:12½:13:14)in

Sleeves

6(6¾:7½:8¾:9½)in

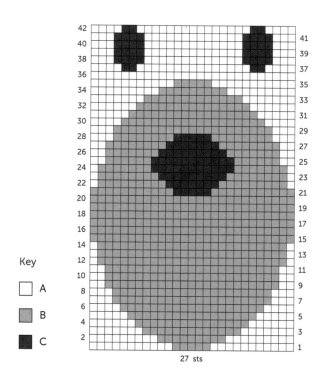

Key

☐ A

▨ B

■ C

27 sts

THE PATTERN

Front

With size US 2 or 3 needles and thumb method, cast on 65(71:77:83:89) sts.
K 6 rows.
Change to size US 3 needles.
Next row (right side): K to end.
Next row: K4, p to last 4 sts, k4.
Rep the last 2 rows 4 times more **.
Beg with a k row, work in st st for a further 10(14:14:34:34) rows.
Place chart
Color change on a slant to the right (page 148)
Color change on a slant to the left (page 148)
Vertical color change (page 149)
1st row (right side):
K19(22:25:28:31), k across 27 sts of 1st row of chart, k19(22:25:28:31).
2nd row: P19(22:25:28:31), p across 27 sts of 2nd row of chart, p19(22:25:28:31).
These 2 rows set the position of the chart. Cont to work from chart until all 42 rows have been completed.
Cont in st st in A only, until front measures 8¼(9:10:11:12½)in from cast-on edge, ending with a k row.
Next row (wrong side):
P16(18:20:22:24), k33(35:37:39:41), p16(18:20:22:24).
Next row: K to end.
Rep the last 2 rows once more.
Shape neck

Next row (wrong side):
P16(18:20:22:24), k4, bind off 25(27:29:31:33) knitwise, with 1 st on needle after bind off, k next 3 sts, p16(18:20:22:24).
Work on the last set of 20(22:24:26:28) sts for left side of neck.
Next row (right side):
K20(22:24:26:28).
Next row: K4, p16(18:20:22:24).
Next row: K to end.
Rep the last 2 rows 5(5:5:6:6) times more.
Buttonhole band
K 1 row.
Next row (right side): K6(7:8:9:10), yf, k2tog, k8(9:10:11:12), yf, k2tog, k2.
K 2 rows.
Bind off knitwise on wrong side.
With right side facing, rejoin yarn to rem 20(22:24:26:28) sts, k to end.
Next row: P16(18:20:22:24), k4.
Next row: K to end.
Rep the last 2 rows 5(5:5:6:6) times more.
Buttonhole band
K 1 row.
Next row (right side): K2, k2tog, yf, k8(9:10:11:12), k2tog, yf, k6(7:8:9:10).
K 2 rows.
Bind off knitwise on wrong side.

Back

Work as given for front to **.
Beg with a k row, work in st st until back measures 9(10:10¼:12:13½) in from cast-on edge, ending with a k row.
Next row: P16(18:20:22:24), k33(35:37:39:41), p16(18:20:22:24).
Next row: K to end.
Rep the last 2 rows once more.
Shape neck
Next row (wrong side):
P16(18:20:22:24), k4, bind off 25(27:29:31:33) knitwise, with 1 st on needle after bind off, k next 3 sts, p16(18:20:22:22:24).
Work on the last set of 20(22:24:26:28) sts for right side of neck.
Next row: K20(22:24:26:28).
Next row: K4, p16(18:20:22:24).
Next row: K to end.
Rep the last 2 rows 2(2:2:3:3) times more.
Button band
K 4 rows.
Bind off knitwise on wrong side.
With right side facing, rejoin yarn to rem 20(22:24:26:28) sts, k to end.
Next row: P16(18:20:22:24), k4.
Next row: K to end.
Rep the last 2 rows 2(2:2:3:3) times more.
Button band
K 4 rows.
Bind off knitwise on wrong side.

Sleeves

(Make 2)

With size US 2 or 3 needles and thumb method, cast on 34(36:38:40:42) sts.

K 6 rows.

Change to size US 3 needles.

Beg with a k row, work in st st.

Work 2 rows.

Inc row: K3, m1, k to last 3 sts, m1, k3.

Work 3 rows.

Rep the last 4 rows 8(10:12:14:16) times more and the inc row again. *54(60:66:72:78) sts*

Cont straight until sleeve measures 6(6¾:7½:8¾:9½)in from cast-on edge, ending with a p row.

Bind off.

To make up

Weave in all intarsia ends.

Sewing in intarsia or stripe ends (page 149)

Lap buttonhole bands over button bands and catch together at outside edge.

With center of bound-off edge of sleeve to shoulder, sew on sleeves.

Join sleeve seams.

Join side seams to top of garter st side edges.

Sew on buttons.

THE TECHNIQUES

Swiss darning

This technique is also referred to as "duplicate stitch" and is worked on stockinette stitch using the same weight yarn as the knitted fabric so that it covers the stitch underneath. You can use this stitch to decorate your knitting, but also to hide mistakes in colorwork, or to provide extra color definition. Try out a motif on a swatch before committing yourself to it on your actual project.

Working horizontally

1 Thread a blunt-tipped sewing needle with yarn the same weight as that used to knit with, and work from right to left. From the back, bring the needle out at the base of a knitted stitch to be embroidered. Pass the needle around the top of the stitch, going under the "legs" of the stitch above.

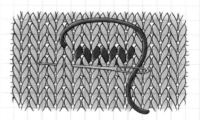

2 Insert the needle back through the base of the same stitch and pull the yarn gently taut, so covering the knitted stitch completely. Bring the needle through at the base of the next stitch to the left.

Working vertically

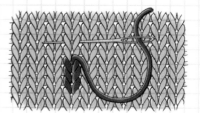

1 Work from bottom to top. From the back, bring the needle out at the base of a knitted stitch to be embroidered. Pass the needle around the top of the stitch, going under the "legs" of the stitch above.

2 Insert the needle back through the base of the same stitch and pull the yarn gently taut, so covering the knitted stitch completely. Bring the needle through at the base of the stitch above.

Color change on a slant to the right

Use this method when the line of the new color is moving across and up to the right on the right side of the work. You can see more clearly how the two yarns interlink on the back on the purl row illustrations.

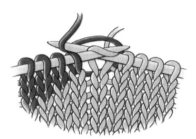

1 On a knit row, work to the last but one stitch in the old color (beige in this example). Insert the right-hand needle knitwise into the last stitch, then bring the new color (brown in this example) across under the old color, wrap it around the tip of the right-hand needle, and knit the stitch in the new color.

2 On a purl row, work to the last stitch in the new color (brown in this example), and knit the next stitch in the old color. Insert the right-hand needle purlwise into the next stitch on the left-hand needle, then bring the old color (beige in this example) up under the new color, and purl the stitch in the old color.

Color change on a slant to the left

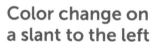

This is the method when the line of the new color is moving across and up to the left on the right side of the work. It is a slightly different procedure for the knit and purl rows than on the slant to the right, but the colors end up linked in the same way on the back.

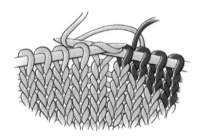

1 On a knit row, work to the last stitch in the new color (brown in this example) and knit the next stitch in the old color. Insert the right-hand needle knitwise into the next stitch on the left-hand needle, then bring the old color (beige in this example) up from under the new color, and knit the stitch in the old color.

2 On a purl row, work to the last but one stitch in the old color (beige in this example). Insert the right-hand needle purlwise into the last stitch, then bring the new color (brown in this example) across under the old color, wrap it around the tip of the right-hand needle, and purl the stitch in the new color.

Vertical color change

Vertical lines require careful tensioning and linking of the two yarn colors because they are prone either to being loose or, for the knit and purl stitches, to varying in size, thus making stitches larger and smaller on alternate rows. Tug the working ends of yarn after making the stitches where the yarns are linked, and make sure your tension in the knit and the purl rows is the same.

1 On a knit row, work to the last stitch in the old color (beige in this example). Bring the new color (brown in this example) under the old color and knit the next stitch firmly.

2 On a purl row, work to the last stitch in the old color (beige in this example). Bring the new color (brown in this example) under the old color and purl the next stitch firmly.

Sewing in intarsia or stripe ends

If you find it difficult to obtain very neat stitches at the color changes in intarsia, you may find that you can fix the stitches when you sew in the ends, as you can fill gaps or tighten stitches at the same time. If you have small motifs that use quite a few colors, do not be tempted to run ends along the main part of the work as it will make the fabric look uneven; always sew in ends along the contrast color at the color changes.

1 Thread a blunt-tipped sewing needle with one end of yarn at a time. Weave the needle up and down through the backs of three or four stitches that are the same color as the end, and pull the end through, keeping it at the same tension as the knitted stitches.

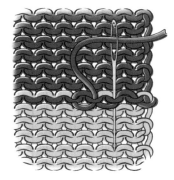

2 Weave the needle back through the stitches in the opposite direction, as shown, pushing it through the yarn to split it. This will help stop the ends working free. Trim the end close to the knitting.

NELLIE THE ELEPHANT

I love knitted toys; they have an old-fashioned look to them and every one is unique depending on how you knit them, stuff them, and embroider their features. Nellie the elephant, named after my daughter of course, is adorable.

Measurements
Approximately 5in high

Materials
2 x 1¾oz (50g) balls of Debbie Bliss Cashmerino Aran in Stone 27 and oddments of black yarn for embroidery
Pair of size US 6 knitting needles
Washable toy stuffing

Gauge
21 sts and 44 rows to 4in square over garter st, using size US 6 needles

Abbreviations
k2tog tbl knit two stitches together through the back loops
psso pass slipped stitch over
sl slip
Also see page 19

Note
The elephant is worked throughout in garter st (k every row).
Pattern note: Shaped pieces (page 152)

Upper body

Cast on 40 sts.
Place a marker on the center of cast-on edge.
K 1 row.

Shape back legs
Cast on 3 sts at beg of next 6 rows. *58 sts*
K 10 rows.
Bind off 3 sts at beg of next 6 rows. *40 sts*
K 8 rows.

Shape front legs
Cast on 3 sts at beg of next 6 rows. *58 sts*
K 8 rows.
Bind off 3 sts at beg of next 6 rows. *40 sts*
K 4 rows.

Shape head
Next row: K to last 6 sts, turn.
Next row: Sl 1, k to last 6 sts, turn.
Next row: Sl 1, k to last 7 sts, k2tog, turn.
Next row: Sl 1, k26, k2tog, turn.
Rep the last row until all sts at each end have been taken into work and 28 sts rem.
Next row: K to last 6 sts, turn.
Next row: Sl 1, k to last 6 sts, turn.
Next row: Sl 1, k14, k2tog, turn.
Rep the last row until all sts at each end have been taken into work and 16 sts rem.
K 24 rows.
Cut yarn, thread through rem sts, pull up and secure.

Body underside

Cast on 3 sts.
Place a marker on the center st.
K 1 row.
Inc 1 st at each end of next 2 rows. *7 sts*
K 1 row.
Inc 1 st at each end of next row. *9 sts*
K 18 rows.
Dec 1 st at each end of next row. *7 sts*
K 4 rows.

Shape back legs
Cast on 3 sts at beg of next row. *10 sts*
Next row: Cast on 3 sts, k3, k2tog tbl, k3, k2tog, k3. *11 sts*
Knit two together through back loops (page 155)
Cast on 3 sts at beg of next 2 rows. *17 sts*
Next row: Cast on 3 sts, k9, k2tog tbl, k1, k2tog, k6. *18 sts*
Cast on 3 sts at beg of next row. *21 sts*
K 1 row.
Next row: K9, sl 1, k2tog, psso, k9. *19 sts*
K 4 rows.
Next row: K9, m1, k1, m1, k9. *21 sts*
K 2 rows.
Next row: K9, m1, k3, m1, k9. *23 sts*
Bind off 3 sts at beg of next 2 rows. *17 sts*
Next row: Bind off 3 sts, k next 2 sts, m1, k5, m1, k6. *16 sts*
Bind off 3 sts at beg of next 3 rows. *7 sts*
K 2 rows.
Inc one st at each end of next row. *9 sts*
K 4 rows.

Pattern note: Shaped pieces

Shaped toys are generally worked in several pieces, some of which can seem a bit odd-looking until you put them together. However, follow the written instructions carefully and then construct the toy as explained and the pieces will make sense.

Dec one st at each end of next row.
7 sts
K 2 rows.
Shape front legs
Cast on 3 sts at beg of next row.
10 sts
Next row: Cast on 3 sts, k3,
k2tog tbl, k3, k2tog, k3. *11 sts*
Cast on 3 sts at beg of next 2 rows.
17 sts
Next row: Cast on 3 sts, k9,
k2tog tbl, k1, k2tog, k6. *18 sts*
Cast on 3 sts at beg of next row.
K 1 row.
Next row: K9, sl 1, k2tog, psso, k9.
19 sts
K 2 rows.
Next row: K9, m1, k1, m1, k9. *21 sts*
K 2 rows.
Next row: K9, m1, k3, m1, k9. *23 sts*
Bind off 3 sts at beg of next
2 rows. *17 sts*
Next row: Bind off 3 sts, k2 sts more,
m1, k5, m1, k6. *16 sts*
Bind off 3 sts at beg of next
3 rows. *7 sts*
K 8 rows.
Dec one st at each end of next row
and foll 4th row. *3 sts*
K 3 rows.
K3tog and fasten off.

First ear
Cast on 14 sts.
K 3 rows.
Next row: K11, k2tog, k1. *13 sts*
K 1 row.
Next row: K10, k2tog, k1. *12 sts*
K 1 row.
Next row: K9, k2tog, k1. *11 sts*
K 5 rows.
Next row: K8, k2tog, k1. *10 sts*
Bind off.

Second ear
Cast on 14 sts.
K 3 rows.
Next row: K1, k2tog, k to end. *13 sts*
K 1 row.
Rep the last 2 rows twice more.
11 sts
K 4 rows.
Next row: K1, k2tog, k to end. *10 sts*
Bind off.

Tail
Cast on 18 sts.
Bind off.

To make up
Stitch up the underside of the trunk,
pulling the yarn tight so that the
trunk curls under slightly. Firmly
stuff the trunk, making sure it keeps
it shape. Leaving an opening in
the seam for stuffing, join upper
body to underside, matching legs
and markers, making sure snout
underside fits into the top of the
trunk. Stuff firmly but evenly.
*Pattern note: Stuffing toys
(see opposite)*
Weave in all ends.
Sew on tail and ears.
With black yarn, embroider the eyes.
*Pattern note: Working the eyes
(see opposite)*

Knit two together through back loops

This decrease slants to the left on stockinette stitch, with a rather pronounced sloping strand. It is worked in a similar way to k2tog, but knitting through the backs of the loops makes the decrease slope in the opposite direction and twists the stitches. It is usually abbreviated to "k2tog tbl."

1 From right to left, insert the right hand needle through the backs of the next two stitches on the left-hand needle and knit them together as one, as for k2tog (page 54). You have decreased by one stitch.

Pattern note: Stuffing toys

As knitted fabric, particularly garter stitch, can be very stretchy, toys are generally worked on needles that are smaller than usually recommended for the yarn used. When it comes to adding the stuffing, you need to keep in mind the shape of the finished toy, otherwise you can overstuff and end up with a rather fat, out-of-shape, unrecognizable animal.

Pull the stuffing apart so it is easy to handle and, starting with small pieces, carefully push them into the far corners of the knitting. Then, maintaining the intended shape, continue putting in enough stuffing to fill the piece, but not overstuff it.

Make sure the back legs match each other and the same with the front legs. The head is probably the most important piece as this is the bit you fall in love with, but it might look slightly strange until you have added the ears, so make up the ears first then you can hold them against the head as you stuff it to see if it all works the way you want it to. You can always take all the stuffing out of a piece and start again if it doesn't look right—nothing is set in stone at this point.

Pattern note: Working the eyes

When it comes to adding the eyes, elephants have small eyes when compared with their bodies, so just a few straight stitches worked on top of each other will be fine. It helps if you mark the position of the eyes before starting sewing.

I always embroider features on toys rather than use sewn-on eyes, which can be easily pulled off and swallowed.

RESOURCES

All your favorite Debbie Bliss yarns and patterns are now available exclusively from LoveCrafts, the online home for makers across the world. With thousands of yarns, patterns, and a global community of makers to connect with, LoveCrafts has everything you need to start your next knitting project!

Explore knitting and crochet patterns by top designers, your favorite yarn brands, and an incredible range of needles and accessories. Learn new skills with LoveCrafts' online tutorials, discover the latest craft trends, and enjoy exciting special offers, every day.

LoveCrafts ships worldwide and has dedicated websites for the US, UK, Australia, and Germany, plus expert help from Smiles, a yarn-loving customer service team.

Visit either LoveKnitting.com, LoveCrochet.com or LoveCrafts.com to start your next project.

INDEX

ACKNOWLEDGMENTS

This book would not have happened without the support of the following amazing people:

Kate Haxell, who has been the most incredible guide throughout the process of putting this book together, for her usual invaluable input, patience, and encouragement. Harriet Butt, at Quadrille, who had faith in the project and commissioned the idea. Katherine Keeble for the lovely design and layout.

Ola Smit for the most beautiful photography. Mia Pejcinovic for her perfect styling and inspiration. Penny Hill for pattern writing and knitting almost all of the knits!

All at LoveCrafts who had faith in the brand.

Knitters everywhere, both new and returning, who encourage others to knit and ensure the craft continues for future generations to enjoy.

Publishing Director Sarah Lavelle
Jnr Commissioning Editor Harriet Butt
Editor Kate Haxell
Designer Katherine Keeble
Photographer Ola Smit
Prop Stylist Mia Pejcinovic
Illustrator Cathy Brear
Production Director Vincent Smith
Production Controller Tom Moore

Bibliographical Note
This Dover edition, first published in 2019, is an unabridged republication of the work published as *First Knits* in 2019 by Quadrille, an imprint of Hardie Grant Publishing.

International Standard Book Number
ISBN-13: 978-0-486-83745-1
ISBN-10: 0-486-83745-9

Printed in China
83745901   2019
www.doverpublications.com